Harold R Foster

Prince Valiant

POCKET IN BACK

COMPRISING PAGES 139 THROUGH 184

The Menace Of The Hun

FANTAGRAPHICS BOOKS

ABOUT THIS EDITION:

Produced in cooperation with the Danish publisher
Interpresse and several other publishers around the world,
this new edition of *PRINCE VALIANT* is intended to be the
definitive compilation of Hal Foster's masterpiece.

In addition to this volume, Fantagraphics Books has in stock
six more collections of Foster's *Prince Valiant* work (Vols. 1-3,
29-31). Future releases will continue reprinting the earlier
material (from 1939 through the end of the 1950s); once the
series has "caught up" with its earlier releases, those will be
reprinted, or (if they are still in print) skipped in order to
complete the collection with the final era (late 1960s through
1982, when Foster handed over the strip to John Cullen
Murphy). The ultimate goal is to have all 40 volumes in
print simultaneously, making available the entirety of Hal
Foster's 45-year epic.

ABOUT THE PUBLISHER:

FANTAGRAPHICS BOOKS has dedicated itself to bringing
readers the finest in comic book and comic strip material,
both new and old. Its "classics" division includes the *The
Complete E.C. Segar Popeye* and *The Complete Little Nemo*. Its
"modern" division is responsible for such works as Yellow
Kid Award-winner *Love and Rockets* by Los Bros. Hernandez,
Peter Bagge's *Neat Stuff*, the American edition of Jose Munoz
and Carlos Sampayo's *Sinner*, and *The Complete R. Crumb
Comics*. See the back cover for a complete listing.

PREVIOUS VOLUMES IN THIS SERIES:

PRINCE VALIANT, Volume 4
"The Menace of the Hun"
comprising pages 139 (October 7, 1939) through 184 (August 20, 1940)
Published by Fantagraphics Books, 1800 Bridgegate Street Suite 101, Westlake Village, CA 91361
Editorial Co-Ordinator: Helle Nielsen
Colored by Monte Serra, Bardon Art
Cover inked by Gorm Transgaard and colored by Søren Håkansson
Fantagraphics Books staff: Kim Thompson & Doug Erb
Copyright © 1988 King Features Syndicate, Inc., Bull's, Interpresse, and Fantagraphics Books, Inc.
Printed in Italy
ISBN 0-930193-49-0
First printing: November, 1988

TRISTRAM
SAVE THIS STAMP

Prince Valiant

IN THE DAYS OF
KING ARTHUR
BY
HAROLD R FOSTER

KALLA KHAN
SAVE THIS STAMP

Synopsis: UNDER PRINCE VALIANT'S DARING LEADERSHIP THE "LEGION OF HUN-HUNTERS" HAS STRUCK AGAIN AND AGAIN AS THE HUNS CROSS THE PASS; RUNNING OFF THEIR HORSES, THEIR PLUNDER AND THEIR SUPPLIES WITH NEVER A CHANCE TO STRIKE BACK AT THEIR NIMBLE FOE. THE HUNS ARE LEFT TO STARVE IN A WILDERNESS OF THEIR OWN MAKING.

THE RAGE OF KALLA KHAN IS TERRIBLE AS THE FAMISHED SURVIVORS STRAGGLE BACK INTO PANNONIA WITH TIDINGS OF STILL MORE DEFEATS.

THE KHAN SUMMONS "KARNAK, THE FEROCIOUS," AND SAYS; "TAKE AN ARMY, CLEAR THE PASS AND FORTIFY IT. TWO MOONS FROM TO-DAY RETURN WITH THE HEAD OF PRINCE VALIANT!"

"YONDER ARE TWO STAKES.... ON ONE IS THE HEAD OF A DEFEATED GENERAL. THE OTHER IS FOR THE HEAD OF PRINCE VALIANT..... OR YOUR OWN!"

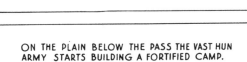

ON THE PLAIN BELOW THE PASS THE VAST HUN ARMY STARTS BUILDING A FORTIFIED CAMP.

BUT NEWS OF VAL'S ASTOUNDING SUCCESS HAS SPREAD FAR AND WIDE AND HIS ARMY GROWS. EVEN SLY VALENTINIAN SENDS 500 ARMED AND MOUNTED KNIGHTS FROM ROME ......

...... AND FROM SPAIN THE KING SENDS A THOUSAND HARD-FIGHTING VISIGOTHS WITH ARMS AND MONEY.

BUT, BEST OF ALL, FROM KING ARTHUR'S COURT IN FAR-OFF BRITAIN, COME TWO BATTERED KNIGHTS ERRANT.... MIGHTY TRISTRAM AND MERRY SIR GAWAIN!

KARNAK
SAVE THIS STAMP

TRISTRAM SEEKING IN HARDSHIP AND ADVENTURE TO FORGET FAIR ISOLDE AND GAWAIN TO ESCAPE KING ARTHUR'S DISPLEASURE AT HIS MISCHIEF.

139 - 10-8-39

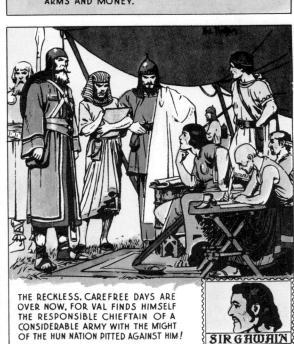

THE RECKLESS, CAREFREE DAYS ARE OVER NOW, FOR VAL FINDS HIMSELF THE RESPONSIBLE CHIEFTAIN OF A CONSIDERABLE ARMY WITH THE MIGHT OF THE HUN NATION PITTED AGAINST HIM!

NEXT WEEK— **TREACHERY!**

SIR GAWAIN
SAVE THIS STAMP

R0012630594

PANDARIS SAVE THIS STAMP

Prince Valiant

IN THE DAYS OF
KING ARTHUR
BY
HAROLD R FOSTER

THE PASS SAVE THIS STAMP

Synopsis: THE RAPIDLY GROWING FORCES UNDER PRINCE VALIANT'S LEADERSHIP HOLD THE PASS, BUT IN THE PLAIN BELOW THE HUNS' VAST ARMY HAS BUILT A STRONGLY FORTIFIED BASE AND MORE MEN AND SUPPLIES ARRIVE DAILY.

HUN SCOUTS TRY DESPERATELY TO FIND OUT THE STRENGTH OF THE "HUN-HUNTERS."

IN THE EXCITEMENT OF THESE SKIRMISHES VAL FORGETS HIS CARES, AND ONCE AGAIN GOES CRASHING INTO THE FRAY, SIDE BY SIDE WITH TRISTRAM AND GAWAIN!

BUT SPIES ARE BEING FOUND IN GREAT NUMBERS, COMING UP BEHIND THEM FROM THE FAR SIDE OF THE PASS — FROM A CAPTURED OFFICER VAL LEARNS THE CAUSE.....

...TWO DAYS' RIDE TO THE SOUTH IS A PASS GUARDED BY THE BEAUTIFUL WALLED CITY OF PANDARIS. DUKE CESARIO HELD THE PASS AGAINST THE HUN, BUT HIS COUSIN, PISCARO, AIDED BY TREACHERY AND THE HUNS, IMPRISONS CESARIO, SETS HIMSELF UP AS TYRANT AND OPENS THE PASS TO THE BARBARIANS.

LOOKING DOWN UPON THEIR ENEMY'S PREPARATIONS, THEY ESTIMATE THAT IT WILL BE TWO MOONS BEFORE THEY ARE READY TO ATTACK. WITH THE ODDS ALREADY 20 TO 1 AGAINST THEM, THE "HUN-HUNTERS'" POSITION WILL BE HOPELESS IF THEY ARE ATTACKED FROM THE REAR ALSO.

HAL FOSTER

140. 10-15-39

Copr. 1939, King Features Syndicate, Inc. World rights reserved.

DESPITE THE OBJECTIONS OF HIS COUNCIL, VAL SETS OUT FOR PANDARIS WITH A FORCE CONSISTING ONLY OF NIMBLE SLITH AND LONG-EARED SOCRATES!

NEXT WEEK-
PANDARIS!

GUIDO
SAVE THIS STAMP

Prince Valiant

IN THE DAYS OF
KING ARTHUR
BY
HAROLD R FOSTER

GATEKEEPER
SAVE THIS STAMP

Synopsis: THE BEAUTIFUL WHITE-WALLED CITY OF PANDARIS STOOD GUARD OVER THE SOUTHERN PASS SO LONG AS BRAVE DUKE CESARIO REIGNED. BUT THE TREACHERY OF HIS COUSIN, PISCARO, OVERTHREW CESARIO AND NOW THE HUNS SWARM THROUGH TO ATTACK THE "HUN-HUNTERS" FROM BEHIND. VAL AND SLITH SET OUT FOR PANDARIS.

A BITING WIND IS MOANING THROUGH THE HIGH PASS AND THEY CROSS IN SAFETY, OBSCURED BY THE SWIRLING SNOW.

IN THE FRIENDLY DARKNESS THEY DRIFT SILENTLY PAST THE SMALL HUN ENCAMPMENTS ON THE FAR SIDE OF THE PASS.

SEVERAL MILES FROM PANDARIS VAL HALTS AT THE HOME OF ONE GUIDO, A FAITHFUL FRIEND OF CESARIO, FOR REST AND INFORMATION.

"PISCARO IS A CRUEL TYRANT, WEAK AND VICIOUS. THE PEOPLE OF PANDARIS WOULD RESTORE BRAVE CESARIO TO POWER, BUT THEIR CITY IS FILLED WITH HUNS AND HE WHO RAISES HIS VOICE AGAINST PISCARO IS SWIFTLY MURDERED."

DRESSED AS PEDDLERS, VAL, SLITH AND SOCRATES APPROACH THE FAIR CITY, ITS SPIRES AND DOMES GLEAMING IN THE SUNLIGHT.

"WHAT IS YOUR BUSINESS WITHIN OUR CITY?" DEMANDS THE OFFICER AT THE GATE. "WE ARE MERCHANTS COME TO CHEAT THE HUNS," ANSWERS VAL BOLDLY. LOOKING CAUTIOUSLY AROUND, THE OFFICER WHISPERS. "PASS, FRIEND!"

PISCARO
SAVE THIS STAMP

WITHIN THE CITY IS THE BROODING SILENCE OF AN UNHAPPY PEOPLE. THE TWO FRIENDS ARE MOVING TOWARD THE PALACE, WHEN TRUMPETS SOUND.....

Nr. 1939, King Features Syndicate, Inc., World rights reserved.
141 10-22-39

AND THE BRUTAL SOLDIERS CLEAR A PATH AMONG THE PEOPLE, AS THE DUKE RIDES FORTH!

NEXT WEEK—
VAL'S DEFIANCE!

CESARIO
SAVE THIS STAMP

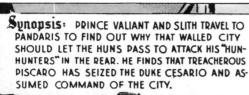

PISCARO'S GUARDS — SAVE THIS STAMP

SOLDIER OF PANDARIS — SAVE THIS STAMP

Synopsis: PRINCE VALIANT AND SLITH TRAVEL TO PANDARIS TO FIND OUT WHY THAT WALLED CITY SHOULD LET THE HUNS PASS TO ATTACK HIS "HUN-HUNTERS" IN THE REAR. HE FINDS THAT TREACHEROUS PISCARO HAS SEIZED THE DUKE CESARIO AND AS-SUMED COMMAND OF THE CITY.

"KNEEL IN THE DUST, SONS OF DOGS. HIS HIGHNESS APPROACHES!" CRY THE SOLDIERS, AS THEY CLEAR A PATH WITH THEIR RODS

THE FALSE DUKE RIDES BY, DAINTILY WAVING A PERFUMED TASSEL BEFORE HIS WEAK, VINDICTIVE FACE.

"KNEEL, SIR," WHISPER THE CITIZENS. "IT IS DEATH MOST TERRIBLE TO OFFEND THE DUKE." BUT VAL IS A PRINCE AND KNIGHT OF THE ROUND TABLE AND WILL KNEEL TO NO SUCH TYRANT! "I'VE SEEN BETTER MEN IN MY FATHER'S STABLES!" QUOTH HE.

THE SOMBER EYE OF THE TYRANT FALLS ON THE ERECT FIGURE OF THE PRINCE AND HIS FACE FLUSHES WITH RAGE. "BREAK HIS LEGS THAT HE MAY BE GLAD TO KNEEL," HE COMMANDS.

"THANKS FOR REMINDING ME OF MY LEGS," SHOUTS VAL AND PROMPTLY USES THEM.

HE IS RAPIDLY OUTRUNNING HIS PURSUERS WHEN, BY ILL LUCK, HE DODGES INTO A BLIND STREET FROM WHICH THERE IS NO OUTLET.

THE NOISE OF PURSUIT IS DRAWING DESPERATELY NEAR WHEN SUDDENLY HE IS SEIZED BY A STRONG HAND AND JERKED INTO A DOORWAY.

142 IQ-29-39   Copr. 1939, King Features Syndicate, Inc., World rights reserved.

VAL WHIPS OUT HIS READY DAGGER, BUT A CALM VOICE SAYS: "WILL YOU TRUST YOURSELF TO ME OR TO THE SOLDIERS OUTSIDE?"

NEXT WEEK—
THE "LIBERATORS"

PANDARIS SOLDIER — SAVE THIS STAMP

PISCARO'S GUARDS — SAVE THIS STAMP

"LIBERATOR"
SAVE THIS STAMP

Prince Valiant
IN THE DAYS OF KING ARTHUR
BY HAROLD R FOSTER

"LIBERATOR"
SAVE THIS STAMP

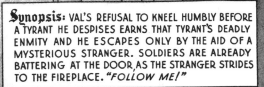

Synopsis: VAL'S REFUSAL TO KNEEL HUMBLY BEFORE A TYRANT HE DESPISES EARNS THAT TYRANT'S DEADLY ENMITY AND HE ESCAPES ONLY BY THE AID OF A MYSTERIOUS STRANGER. SOLDIERS ARE ALREADY BATTERING AT THE DOOR, AS THE STRANGER STRIDES TO THE FIREPLACE. "FOLLOW ME!"

HE DISAPPEARS UPWARD IN THE DARKNESS AND VAL QUICKLY FOLLOWS—HIS GROPING HANDS FIND THE NICHES AND HE MOUNTS RAPIDLY.

THEY EMERGE INTO THE ADJOINING HOUSE. "THIS IS THE SECRET MEETING-PLACE OF THE 'LIBERATORS.' I TRUST YOUR HATRED OF PISCARO WILL MAKE YOU ONE OF US."

THE "LIBERATORS" ARE FAITHFUL FRIENDS OF DUKE CESARIO, FORCED BY PISCARO'S WEAK FEROCITY TO SEEK SAFETY IN DISGUISE AND HIDING.... AND IN THEIR HIDING-PLACES THEY PLOT.

VAL LEARNS THAT THE CITIZENS LOATHE THE CRUEL PISCARO, BUT THE MENACING SHADOW OF THE HUN KEEPS THEM COWED. ONLY THROUGH THE DEATH OF PISCARO AND LIBERATION OF DUKE CESARIO CAN VAL EXPECT HELP FOR HIS TROOPS.

ALL THROUGH THE DAY AND INTO THE NIGHT THE SOLDIERS SEARCH FOR PRINCE VALIANT, FOR THEY FEAR THEIR MASTER'S WRATH IF THEY FAIL.

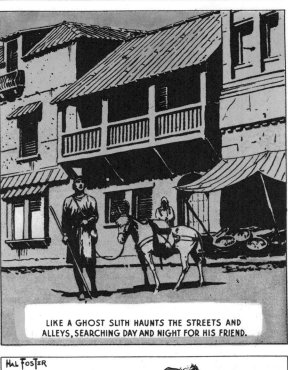

LIKE A GHOST SLITH HAUNTS THE STREETS AND ALLEYS, SEARCHING DAY AND NIGHT FOR HIS FRIEND.

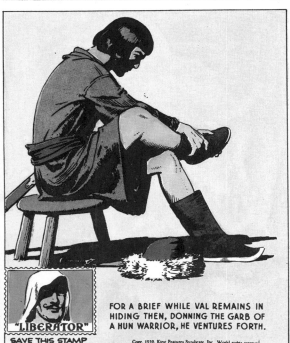

FOR A BRIEF WHILE VAL REMAINS IN HIDING THEN, DONNING THE GARB OF A HUN WARRIOR, HE VENTURES FORTH.

Copr. 1939, King Features Syndicate, Inc., World rights reserved.

BUT, NO MATTER WHAT CLOTHES HE WEARS, THERE IS ONE THING HE CANNOT DISGUISE; HE IS A KING'S SON AND LOOKS IT EVERY INCH!

143 11-5-39

HAL FOSTER

HE IS RECOGNIZED IMMEDIATELY, OVER-POWERED AND DRAGGED OFF TO THE PALACE... AND PISCARO'S VENGEANCE!

NEXT WEEK—
PISCARO'S TORTURE ROOM!

"LIBERATOR"
SAVE THIS STAMP

A TORMENTOR
SAVE THIS STAMP

Prince Valiant

IN THE DAYS OF
KING ARTHUR
BY
HAROLD R FOSTER

A TORTURER
SAVE THIS STAMP

Synopsis: THE EVIL PISCARO HAS TAKEN THE CITY PANDARIS FROM DUKE CESARIO THROUGH TREACHERY AND THE HUNS' AID. CESARIO IS THROWN INTO PRISON AND THE HUNS ARE FREE TO ATTACK VAL'S TROOPS FROM THE REAR. VAL HAS EARNED THE ENMITY OF PISCARO.

A DISGUISE CANNOT HIDE HIS PRINCELY BEARING; VAL IS RECOGNIZED AND QUICKLY CAPTURED.

IN A ROOM DRUGGED WITH THE VAPOR OF PERFUME AND INCENSE VAL STANDS BEFORE PISCARO AND MEETS THE UNBLINKING HATRED IN HIS EYES.

"SO - THEY HAVE BROUGHT YOU TO ME AT LAST! EVERYONE FEARS ME....ONLY YOU DEFY ME....BUT YOU HAVE NOT YET VISITED MY TORTURE CHAMBER. SOON YOU WILL WHIMPER FOR THE RELIEF OF DEATH." AND PISCARO SNICKERS.

VAL IS DRAGGED BRUTALLY DOWN TO A DUNGEON CELL......

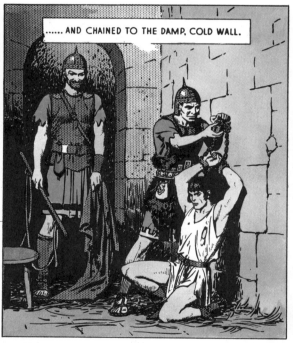

...... AND CHAINED TO THE DAMP, COLD WALL.

DEATH AND HORROR LURK IN THE VERY AIR OF THIS GRUESOME PLACE. VAL'S MIND IS BUSY WITH PLANS FOR ESCAPE WHEN HE IS STARTLED BY A VOICE.

CESARIO
SAVE THIS STAMP

THROUGH A SMALL WINDOW BETWEEN THE CELLS PEERS A PALE FACE. »I AM DUKE CESARIO.» HE WHISPERS. »THE SCREAMS OF PISCARO'S VICTIMS ARE DRIVING ME MAD, IS THERE ANY HOPE OF RESCUE?»

VAL TELLS HIM OF THE "LIBERATORS" WHILE A SPY LISTENS OUTSIDE. FOR THESE WINDOWS BETWEEN THE CELLS ARE FOR THE PURPOSE OF ENCOURAGING TALK.

HAL FOSTER

144 11-12-39

AT FIRST VAL'S NIMBLE MIND IS BUSY WITH SCHEMES FOR ESCAPE, BUT AS THE DAYS DRAG INTO WEEKS HE BECOMES NUMBED WITH MISERY. PISCARO'S VOICE AWAKENS HIM: "YOUR TIME HAS COME!"

NEXT WEEK-
THE RACK!

PISCARO
SAVE THIS STAMP

Synopsis: TO PREVENT HIS "LEGION OF HUN-HUNTERS" FROM BEING SURROUNDED, VAL FINDS IT NECESSARY TO RESCUE THE DUKE CESARIO FROM THE HANDS OF TREACHEROUS PISCARO. UNFORTUNATELY, PRINCE VALIANT, HIMSELF, FALLS INTO PISCARO'S POWER AND HAS SPENT TWO WEEKS CRUELLY CHAINED IN A FILTHY CELL.

"AND NOW THE TIME HAS COME FOR MY SWEET REVENGE," SAYS PISCARO, RUBBING HIS COLD HANDS SOFTLY TOGETHER.

THE TORMENTORS STRETCH VAL'S STRONG YOUNG BODY UPON THE RACK AND DRAW THE CHAINS TIGHT, WHILE PISCARO SNICKERS.

"NOW TELL ME WHO THE 'LIBERATORS ARE.... TELL ME WHO PLOTS AGAINST ME, BEFORE YOUR BONES CRACK. NAME THOSE WHO WOULD FREE CESARIO, OR SLOWLY WILL I TEAR YOUR BEAUTIFUL BODY ASUNDER."

THE MERCILESS TORMENTORS BEAR DOWN ON THEIR LEVERS. THERE COMES A HORRIBLE SNAP. VAL SCREAMS, "I'LL TELL, OH! I'LL TELL!".. HE MOANS AND FAINTS.

"CLUMSY FOOLS!" SHRIEKS PISCARO, "IF YOU HAVE KILLED HIM IT IS THE RACK FOR BOTH OF YOU! REVIVE HIM AND WHEN HE CAN TALK, CALL ME."

LATER, WHEN THEY CALL HIM, HE SAYS, "AFTER I HAVE HIS CONFESSION YOU MAY BEAT HIM TO DEATH."

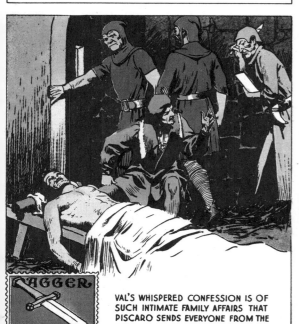

VAL'S WHISPERED CONFESSION IS OF SUCH INTIMATE FAMILY AFFAIRS THAT PISCARO SENDS EVERYONE FROM THE CELL.

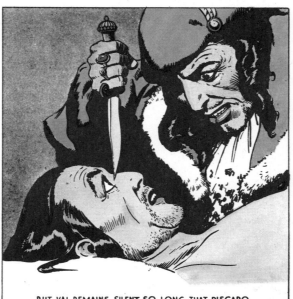

BUT VAL REMAINS SILENT SO LONG THAT PISCARO DRAWS HIS DAGGER AND LEANS THREATENINGLY OVER HIS BROKEN AND HELPLESS VICTIM.

HELPLESS? WELL, NOT QUITE... FOR TWO STRONG HANDS SEIZE HIM IN A VICE-LIKE GRIP AND HE IS BORNE SILENTLY TO THE FLOOR.

NEXT WEEK—
A NEW PISCARO.

Copr. 1939, King Features Syndicate, Inc. World rights reserved.

145 11-19-39

SAXON CLEAVER
SAVE THIS STAMP

VIKING BATTLE AXE
SAVE THIS STAMP

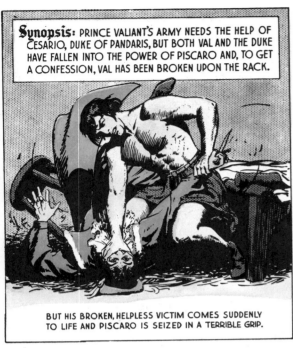

Synopsis: PRINCE VALIANT'S ARMY NEEDS THE HELP OF CESARIO, DUKE OF PANDARIS, BUT BOTH VAL AND THE DUKE HAVE FALLEN INTO THE POWER OF PISCARO AND, TO GET A CONFESSION, VAL HAS BEEN BROKEN UPON THE RACK.

BUT HIS BROKEN, HELPLESS VICTIM COMES SUDDENLY TO LIFE AND PISCARO IS SEIZED IN A TERRIBLE GRIP.

THE HATRED BORN OF WEEKS OF MISERY GOES INTO THAT ONE SMASHING BLOW

WHEN, FINALLY, PISCARO RETURNS TO CONSCIOUSNESS A GREAT CHANGE HAS TAKEN PLACE—HE HAS HAD A HAIR-CUT, A SHAVE AND A CHANGE OF CLOTHES—HE HAS A BROKEN ARM AND A GREAT FEAR!

"THOUGHT YOU HAD BROKEN ME, DID YOU? TAUNTS VAL. "MY BONES DIDN'T BREAK—I JUST CLICKED MY TEETH AND SNAPPED MY FINGERS.....THE REST WAS ACTING!"

REMOVING THE GAG VAL HITS HIM AGAIN ON THE CHIN TO KEEP HIM QUIET. THEN, IMITATING PISCARO'S MINCING WALK, LEAVES THE DUNGEON.

THROUGH HIS LITTLE WINDOW DUKE CESARIO SEES THE WHOLE ASTONISHING SCENE......EVEN NOW HE CAN HARDLY BELIEVE THAT THE MOANING FIGURE ON THE COT IS NOT VAL.....AND HOPE COMES AGAIN TO THE DUKE.

AXE-MACE
SAVE THIS STAMP

WITH HEAD DOWN VAL QUICKLY MINCES ACROSS THE BRILLIANT HALL AND TO PISCARO'S ROOMS.

"BRING CESARIO HERE, AND CHAIN HIM TO THE WALL!"

146 11-26-39   Copr. 1939, King Features Syndicate, Inc., World rights reserved.

WHEN THEY ARE ALONE, VAL SAYS, "THE PALACE IS FILLED WITH PISCARO'S FRIENDS. I CANNOT LONG REMAIN UNDETECTED, YET I CANNOT ESCAPE. HAVE YOU A PLAN?"
NEXT WEEK—
THE PLAN.

BATTLE-AXE
SAVE-THIS STAMP

Synopsis: VAL TRICKS PISCARO INTO THINKING HIM HELPLESS AND PISCARO ENTERS THE CELL ALONE. VAL LEAVES, DRESSED IN PISCARO'S GARMENTS, WHILE THE PETTY TYRANT STAYS TO FACE THE DOOM HE HAS ORDERED FOR VAL. STILL POSING AS PISCARO, VAL ORDERS THE REAL DUKE BROUGHT FROM THE DUNGEON AND CHAINED TO THE WALL

"THE CASTLE IS FILLED WITH PISCARO'S FRIENDS. NOT ONLY MUST WE ESCAPE, BUT YOU MUST ONCE MORE RULE IN THE CITY OF PANDARIS."

"I HAVE IT!.... WE CANNOT GO TO YOUR FRIENDS, BUT WE CAN BRING YOUR FRIENDS TO US!"

"GET BACK IN YOUR CHAINS, CESARIO, WHILE I SUMMON THE GUARDS, AND REMEMBER... I AM PISCARO AND I HAVE FORCED YOU TO BETRAY YOUR FOLLOWERS."

"MY DEAR COUSIN HAS AT LAST DECIDED TO BETRAY HIS FAITHFUL FRIENDS...TAKE DOWN THEIR NAMES AND ARREST THEM. BY TO-MORROW MY RULE WILL BE UN-QUESTIONED!"

"BUT REMEMBER - ARREST EACH ONE SECRETLY AND LOCK THEM UR UNHARMED, IN THE ARMORY."

CREST OF PISCARO

AT THE STROKE OF MIDNIGHT THE ORDER IS QUIETLY CARRIED OUT.

INTO THE GLOOMY, ECHOING ARMORY ARE HERDED ALL WHO HAD REMAINED FAITHFUL TO DUKE CESARIO.

CREST OF CESARIO

PISCARO SAVE THIS STAMP

VAL'S DISGUISE SAVE THIS STAMP

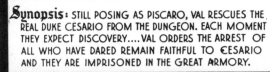

Synopsis: STILL POSING AS PISCARO, VAL RESCUES THE REAL DUKE CESARIO FROM THE DUNGEON. EACH MOMENT THEY EXPECT DISCOVERY....VAL ORDERS THE ARREST OF ALL WHO HAVE DARED REMAIN FAITHFUL TO CESARIO AND THEY ARE IMPRISONED IN THE GREAT ARMORY.

"AH! SIR VALIANT, I SEE YOUR PLAN NOW—IN NO OTHER WAY COULD MY FRIENDS ENTER THIS STRONGHOLD."

THEIR PLANNING IS INTERRUPTED BY THE MASTER OF THE DUNGEONS..."WE HAVE FINISHED WITH PRINCE VALIANT AS YOU DIRECTED, YOUR EXCELLENCY, HE DIED SCREAMING VERY SATISFACTORILY."

"FOOL! I AM PRINCE VALIANT. THAT WAS PISCARO YOU KILLED!"

IN THOSE TWO BLAZING EYES THE MASTER TORTURER READS CLEARLY HIS DOOM—HE LEAPS FOR THE DOOR JUST A SECOND TOO LATE.

"IT IS AN UNPLEASANT FACT THAT YOU AND I SO RESEMBLE THE WORLD'S TWO MEANEST SCOUNDRELS THAT WE CAN ACT THEIR PARTS."

IN AN AGONY OF DESPAIR SLITH WAITS DAY AFTER DAY FOR SOME WORD OF HIS MASTER'S FATE.

AT THE "HUN-HUNTERS" CAMP NO WORD HAS COME FROM THEIR CHIEFTAIN FOR OVER TWO WEEKS. HULTA, THE MESSENGER, QUIETLY SADDLES HIS HORSE AND RIDES FOR PANDARIS.

QUESTIONER SAVE THIS STAMP

HE SOON FINDS THE HAGGARD, SLEEPLESS SLITH AND LEARNS FROM HIM OF VAL'S CAPTURE BY PISCARO.

Copr. 1939, King Features Syndicate, Inc., World rights reserved 148 12-10-39

WITH THE SEEMING RECKLESSNESS OF THE BORN HORSEMAN HULTA SPEEDS BACK TO THE CAMP.

HAL FOSTER

NEXT WEEK— **IN THE ARMORY**

CESARIO'S DISGUISE SAVE THIS STAMP

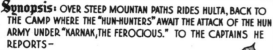

Synopsis: OVER STEEP MOUNTAIN PATHS RIDES HULTA, BACK TO THE CAMP WHERE THE "HUN-HUNTERS" AWAIT THE ATTACK OF THE HUN ARMY UNDER "KARNAK, THE FEROCIOUS." TO THE CAPTAINS HE REPORTS —

"PRINCE VALIANT, OUR FEARLESS LEADER, IS HELD PRISONER BY FALSE DUKE PISCARO, HIS FATE UNKNOWN.... IF WE TURN FROM THE HUN ARMY TO ATTACK PISCARO'S WALLED CITY OF PANDARIS WE WILL BE CAUGHT BETWEEN TWO ENEMIES."

ALL AGREE THAT HULTA SPEAKS TRUE..... BUT LATER THEY SPEAK AS FOLLOWS -- SAYS SIR GAWAIN;- "I BELIEVE I SHALL RIDE TO PANDARIS AND HAVE THIS SWORD SHARPENED," AND TRISTRAM REMARKS:- "SPLENDID WEATHER FOR RIDING, I'LL JOIN YOU!"

TO HIS SECOND IN COMMAND VONDERMAN OF THE FOOT-SOLDIERS SAYS:- "TAKE CHARGE WHILE I LEARN MORE ABOUT HORSEBACK-RIDING!"

CESARIO, THE HORSEMAN REMARKS; "MY WAR-HORSE GROWS STIFF FROM LACK OF EXERCISE, I MUST ATTEND TO IT AT ONCE!"

DE GATIN OF THE ARCHERS SHOUTS; "I GROW WEARY OF THIS WAITING FOR THE HUN ATTACK, I AM OFF FOR A FEW DAYS OF HUNTING!"

BUT YOUNG HULTA, THE MESSENGER, SAYS NOTHING AS USUAL... HE HAS ALREADY LEFT TO JOIN HIS FRIEND, SLITH, IN PANDARIS!

SO IT IS NOT STRANGE THAT THEY ALL MEET ON THE ROAD TO PANDARIS A FEW HOURS LATER!

MEANWHILE, WITHIN THE PALACE, VAL, DISGUISED AS PISCARO AND DUKE CESARIO IN THE GARMENT OF THE LATE CHIEF TORTURER, PREPARE TO PUT THEIR PLAN TO THE TEST.

ORDERING THE ENTIRE PALACE GUARD AS ESCORT, THEY PASS UNDETECTED THROUGH THE CROWDED PALACE INTO THE COURTYARD.

"ARE YOU SURE THE PRISONERS ARE SECURELY CHAINED? HAVE THEY BEEN SEARCHED FOR WEAPONS? THEN GIVE ME THE KEYS THAT I MAY BE SURE."

"MY CHIEF TORTURER WILL HELP ME AMUSE MYSELF WITH MY MANY PRISONERS - WAIT OUTSIDE, READY TO ANSWER MY SLIGHTEST CALL."

149   12-17-39   Copr. 1939, King Features Syndicate, Inc. World rights reserved.

"SPLENDID," GRINS VAL, "ARMS AND ARMOR AND FIFTY OF YOUR GOOD FRIENDS TO USE THEM... TO WORK!"

NEXT WEEK—
HOUSECLEANING.

ROMAN CUIRASS
SAVE THIS STAMP

Prince Valiant

IN THE DAYS OF KING ARTHUR
BY
HAROLD R FOSTER

VIKING CHAINMAIL
SAVE THIS STAMP

Synopsis: MASQUERADING AS PISCARO, SIR VALIANT HAS ORDERED THE ARREST OF ALL WHO ARE LOYAL TO THE REAL DUKE CESARIO. VAL AND CESARIO ARE NOW VISITING THEIR PRISONERS, ALONE, IN THE VAST ARMORY.

"CAUTION YOUR FRIENDS TO ABSOLUTE SILENCE AND THEN REVEAL YOURSELF TO THEM, CESARIO."

WHISPERED GREETINGS WITH THEIR NOBLE LEADER OF OLD, THEN HURRIEDLY EACH ONE ARMS HIMSELF...

"OFFICER, MARCH THE GUARD IN AND FORM AGAINST THE SOUTH WALL."

WITHIN THE DIM BUILDING THEY FIND NOT HELPLESS PRISONERS, BUT FIFTY ARMED KNIGHTS AND THE GRIM-FACED DUKE. "I WILL JUDGE OF YOUR LOYALTY LATER, UNTIL THEN YOU WILL BE LOCKED IN THIS ARMORY."

THE FRIENDS AND FOLLOWERS OF SLY PISCARO ARE STARTLED TO SEE HIM LEAD A TROOP OF FULLY ARMED KNIGHTS ACROSS THE GREAT HALL TO THE DUCAL THRONE.

THERE CESARIO REMOVES HIS HELMET—
"I AM CESARIO, RIGHTFUL DUKE OF PANDARIS—THIS IS THE FAR-FAMED PRINCE VALIANT. THESE ARE MY GOOD FRIENDS... WE HAVE COME TO CLEAN HOUSE!"

GROMAN SCALE MAIL
SAVE THIS STAMP

DOWN THE DUSTY ROAD INTO PANDARIS COMES TRISTRAM, GAWAIN, HULTA, DE GATIN, VONDERMAN AND CESARIO, THE HORSEMAN, TO RESCUE THEIR LEADER OR SEEK VENGEANCE.

THERE WAS NEVER A MORE UNTIDY HOUSECLEANING!

HAL FOSTER

150-12-24-39

Copr. 1939, King Features Syndicate, Inc., World rights reserved

NEXT WEEK—
FROM FRYING PAN TO FIRE!

GROMAN LEATHER MAIL
SAVE THIS STAMP

Prince Valiant
IN THE DAYS OF KING ARTHUR
BY HAROLD R. FOSTER
Registered U. S. Patent Office.

TURK
SAVE THIS STAMP

ARABIAN
SAVE THIS STAMP

Synopsis: KNOWING ONLY THAT PRINCE VALIANT, THEIR GAY LEADER, IS PRISONER IN PISCARO'S PALACE, HIS FRIENDS STAKE THEIR LIVES ON A DESPERATE RESCUE.

ROUSED FROM HIS WEARY VIGIL BEFORE THE PALACE GATE, FAITHFUL SLITH SEES THEM COMING AND SNATCHES HIS WEAPONS FROM SOCRATES' PACK.

THE MEMORY OF CRUEL INJUSTICES LENDS STRENGTH TO THE ARMS OF DUKE CESARIO'S KNIGHTS, AS THEY SWEEP PISCARO'S FOLLOWERS FROM THE PALACE.

AS THEY BREAK IN PANIC TOWARD THE GATE, A WILD BATTLE-CRY IS HEARD AND VAL'S FRIENDS COME CRASHING THROUGH.

THE MORNING'S WORK IS SMARTLY FINISHED AND WEEKS OF ANXIETY ARE FORGOTTEN, AS GOOD FRIENDS MEET AGAIN. *"THERE IS NOTHING LIKE A LITTLE EXERCISE BEFORE LUNCH TO GIVE ONE AN APPETITE,"* REMARKS TRISTRAM, LOOKING ANXIOUSLY OVER THE SLAIN TO SEE IF ANY OF THE KITCHEN STAFF HAD BEEN WASTED.

" PISCARO IS SLAIN, DUKE CESARIO REIGNS. WE ARE FREE AGAIN!"

THE HUNS HEAR AND TREMBLE - FOR UNDER PISCARO'S RULE THEY DID AS THEY PLEASED AND HEAPED INSULT AND INDIGNITY UPON THE HELPLESS CITIZENS.

TOUREG
SAVE THIS STAMP

THEN COMES A NIGHT OF HORROR, AS THE MEN OF PANDARIS TURN ON THEIR SNEERING OPPRESSORS AND HUNT THEM THROUGH THE STREETS.

Hal Foster

NEXT WEEK—
BACK TO DUTY AND A PLAN.

AFRICAN
SAVE THIS STAMP

151 12-31-39   Copr. 1939, King Features Syndicate, Inc. World rights reserved

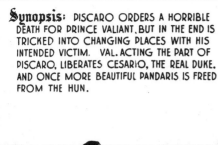

Synopsis: PISCARO ORDERS A HORRIBLE DEATH FOR PRINCE VALIANT, BUT IN THE END IS TRICKED INTO CHANGING PLACES WITH HIS INTENDED VICTIM. VAL. ACTING THE PART OF PISCARO, LIBERATES CESARIO, THE REAL DUKE. AND ONCE MORE BEAUTIFUL PANDARIS IS FREED FROM THE HUN.

THE MENACE OF THE HUN HAS LAIN LIKE AN EVIL SHADOW OVER THE CITY. AND THIS NIGHT. WHILE THE NOBLES FEAST, THE PEOPLE HUNT THEIR SAVAGE OPPRESSORS THROUGH THE DARK STREETS. WHEN THE LONG NIGHT OF HORROR ENDS THERE IS NO LIVING HUN WITHIN THE CITY'S GATES.

"YOU HAVE PUT AN END TO A TERRIBLE NIGHTMARE, SIR VALIANT. ASK WHAT YOU WILL OF ME."

VAL LEARNS THAT 4000 HUNS HAVE COME THROUGH THE PANDARIS PASS TO ATTACK HIS ARMY FROM THE REAR. HALF THIS NUMBER HAVE PERISHED DURING THE NIGHT.........

ALL THE BELLS ARE RINGING JOYOUSLY, THERE IS MUSIC IN THE STREETS AND THE PEOPLE ARE DANCING... FREEDOM AND LAUGHTER HAVE COME AGAIN TO PANDARIS! THROUGH THIS BRIGHT SCENE VAL RIDES TO THE GRIM BUSINESS AHEAD.

"LOAN ME 500 HEAVILY ARMED KNIGHTS AND I WILL SWEEP THIS SIDE OF THE MOUNTAINS CLEAR OF HUNS, AND YOU, CESARIO, LET NO MORE THROUGH THE PASS ABOVE PANDARIS."

Copr. 1940, King Features Syndicate, Inc. World rights reserved

152 1-7-40

NEXT WEEK—
THE INVINCIBLES FALL!

Synopsis: THE GRATEFUL DUKE CESARIO HAS LOANED PRINCE VALIANT 500 KNIGHTS TO DISPERSE THE HUN ARMY THAT MENACES THE REAR OF THE "HUN-HUNTERS." ON THE FAR SIDE OF THE MOUNTAINS VAL'S "LEGION OF HUN-HUNTERS" STILL HOLDS THE PASS IN THE FACE OF THE MAIN HUN ARMY.

TO HIS OFFICERS THE YOUNG PRINCE EXPLAINS HIS PLAN OF ATTACK.... THEY IN TURN FALL BACK AND INSTRUCT THE OTHER KNIGHTS, AS THEY MOVE SWIFTLY FORWARD.

SCOUTS SEE THEM COMING AND SPEED TO THEIR CHIEFTAIN WITH THEIR NEWS.

FOR SIX YEARS THESE BARBARIANS HAVE PILLAGED EUROPE AT WILL WITHOUT DEFEAT --- CONFIDENTLY THEY PREPARE FOR ANOTHER VICTORY.

THE AIR TREMBLES WITH SAVAGE CRIES AND THUNDERING HOOFS, AS THE INVINCIBLE HUN BATTLE FORMATION RUSHES FORWARD,- WINGS WIDE-SPREAD LIKE ENGULFING HORNS.

BUT VAL HAS BEEN SCHOOLED IN BATTLE AT THE COURT OF KING ARTHUR... AT A COMMAND HIS MAIL-CLAD WARRIORS FORM THE TERRIBLE WEDGE AND CHARGE.

NOTHING HUMAN COULD WITHSTAND THAT IRON-CLAD BLOW. THE HUNS' LEFT WING IS SLICED OFF AND CRUMPLES.

MEDIEVAL SADDLE SAVE THIS STAMP

THEN, SWERVING RIGHT AND LEFT THEY SWEEP FURIOUSLY DOWN THE ENEMY LINE... ROLLING IT BACK IN HELPLESS CONFUSION.

VAL SEEKS AND FINDS THE HUN CHIEFTAIN....SOON THEIR BUSINESS TOGETHER IS FINISHED AND VAL GAZES OVER THE STREWN FIELD. GRIMLY, EFFICIENTLY HIS MEN ARE EXTERMINATING THE FLEEING HUNS.

HIGH ON THE PASS THEIR WORK IS COMPLETED AND THEY PART.... VAL AND HIS FRIENDS TO CROSS OVER AND ONCE AGAIN TAKE COMMAND OF THE "LEGION OF HUN-HUNTERS."

NEXT WEEK- **FAMINE**

MEDIEVAL SADDLE SAVE THIS STAMP

Copr. 1940, King Features Syndicate. Inc. World rights reserved

153 1-14-40

Prince Valiant
IN THE DAYS OF KING ARTHUR
BY
Harold R Foster

GUIDO
SAVE THIS STAMP

GATEKEEPER
SAVE THIS STAMP

Synopsis: THREE LONG WEEKS HAVE PASSED SINCE VAL LAST SAW HIS LITTLE "LEGION OF HUN-HUNTERS." IN THE MEANTIME, HE HAS LEARNED ONE GREAT FACT: THE ONCE-INVINCIBLE HUN CAN BE BEATEN!

WHEN THEY COME IN SIGHT OF THE CAMP VAL CRIES OUT IN ASTONISHMENT --- HIS LITTLE BAND HAS GROWN TO AN ARMY, 7000 STRONG.

NEWS OF HIS SUCCESSFUL RAIDS HAS SPREAD THROUGHOUT EUROPE...... THERE COME KNIGHTS ERRANT SEEKING ADVENTURE, BANDITS SEEKING LOOT, DESPOILED NOBLES SEEKING REVENGE AND WARRIORS SEEKING A LEADER WORTH FOLLOWING.

A VAST STORE OF SUPPLIES HAD BEEN TAKEN FROM THE HUNS, BUT HARDLY ENOUGH TO FEED THIS GREAT NUMBER. VAL LEARNS THAT FAMINE IS UPON THEM.

A TERRIBLE RESPONSIBILITY FOR SO YOUNG A LAD - SHOULD HE FAIL TO HOLD THE PASS EUROPE WILL BE AGAIN OVERRUN BY THE HUN.

AT DAWN A PANTING SCOUT ARRIVES, "SIR VALIANT, THE HUNS PREPARE TO ATTACK!"

"OH! FOR A PLAN," CRIES VAL, "A PLAN THAT WILL ENABLE 7000 STARVING CHRISTIANS TO DEFEAT 20,000 HUNS WITH A FORTIFIED CAMP!"

FROM A ROCKY OUTPOST VAL AND SLITH LOOK DOWN ON THE ENEMY CAMP. THERE IS GREAT ACTIVITY AND, THEY JUDGE, THE HUNS WILL MARCH FORTH NEXT DAWN TO SWEEP THE PASS. SUPPLY TRAINS ARE STILL ENTERING THE GATE..... ....."WISH WE COULD ENTER AS EASILY," SAYS SLITH.

FOOTWEAR
SAVE THIS STAMP

HAL FOSTER

"WE CAN!" SHOUTS VAL, "WE WILL!, BY ZEUS, A PLAN! SUMMON THE COUNCIL.... VICTORY MAY YET BE OURS!"

NEXT WEEK—
THE HUNS MARCH.

FOOTWEAR
SAVE THIS STAMP

154 1-21-40

THE KING'S JESTER
DAGONET
SAVE THIS STAMP

Prince Valiant

IN THE DAYS OF KING ARTHUR
BY
HAROLD R FOSTER

Registered U.S. Patent Office.

THE KIN
THE ARMORER
SAVE THIS STAMP

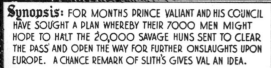

Synopsis: FOR MONTHS PRINCE VALIANT AND HIS COUNCIL HAVE SOUGHT A PLAN WHEREBY THEIR 7000 MEN MIGHT HOPE TO HALT THE 20,000 SAVAGE HUNS SENT TO CLEAR THE PASS AND OPEN THE WAY FOR FURTHER ONSLAUGHTS UPON EUROPE. A CHANCE REMARK OF SLITH'S GIVES VAL AN IDEA.

THE PLAN IS DARING, INSPIRED, DANGEROUS, BUT THEIR DESPERATE PLIGHT CALLS FOR A DES-PERATE PLAN, AND VAL'S ENTHUSIASM FINALLY WINS CONSENT FROM THE COUNCIL.

DEFEAT WILL COST HIM HIS HEAD, SO KARNAK, CHIEFTAIN OF THE HUNS, HAS PROCEEDED CAREFULLY. HIS BASE IS FORTIFIED AND PILED HIGH WITH SUPPLIES.... HIS FIERCE WARRIORS ARE CLAMORING TO BE LOOSED UPON THEIR NIMBLE FOES.

AT DAWN THEY ISSUE FORTH, DRUMS THROBBING, SPEARS WAVING AND SWORDS CLASHING ON SHIELDS.

LIKE A GREAT OCTOPUS THE HUN ARMY MOVES SLOWLY UP THE WIDE VALLEY, ITS FAR-FLUNG ARMS SWEEPING EVERY FOLD AND HOLLOW OF THE ENCIRCLING HILLS.

"GENTLEMEN, THE HUN IS IN FRONT OF US, FAMINE LURKS BEHIND, TO-NIGHT WE BANQUET ROYALLY ON THE LAST OF OUR PROVISIONS..... AND TO-MORROW?.... DEATH OR PLENTY!"

FROM AMONG THE RANKS WILY SLITH CHOOSES ALL THOSE WHO MOST RESEMBLE HUNS, PUTS HUN COSTUMES OVER THEIR ARMOR, THEN, WITH A MYSTERIOUS PACK TRAIN DISAPPEARS SILENTLY INTO THE NIGHT.

SPURS
SAVE THIS STAMP

BY NOON OF THIS, THE SECOND DAY, KARNAK IS WELL UP THE PASS AND STILL NO SIGN OF AN ENEMY. INDEED, THERE IS NO ENEMY, FOR.....

Copr. 1940, King Features Syndicate, Inc.. World rights reserved   155   1-28-40

HAL FOSTER

VAL HAD SAID TO HIS HUN-HUNTERS: "KARNAK'S WOLVES ARE AT THE MOUTH OF OUR CANYON, HULTA WILL LEAD US BY A SECRET WAY TO THE PLAINS BELOW, THERE TO PUT OUR PLAN TO THE TEST."

NEXT WEEK—
VAL INVITES KARNAK TO DINE!

SPURS
SAVE THIS STAMP

FIRE BALL

WIRE GRAPPLES
SAVE THIS STAMP

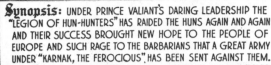

FIRE-THROWER

LEATHER ARMOR
SAVE THIS STAMP

Synopsis: UNDER PRINCE VALIANT'S DARING LEADERSHIP THE "LEGION OF HUN-HUNTERS" HAS RAIDED THE HUNS AGAIN AND AGAIN AND THEIR SUCCESS BROUGHT NEW HOPE TO THE PEOPLE OF EUROPE AND SUCH RAGE TO THE BARBARIANS THAT A GREAT ARMY UNDER "KARNAK, THE FEROCIOUS" HAS BEEN SENT AGAINST THEM.

DUSK OF THE SECOND DAY. HIGH UP NEAR THE TOP OF THE PASS THE HUN ARMY PAUSES..... NO ENEMY HAS YET BEEN SEEN, NOTHING BUT SILENCE AND DESOLATION. AND KARNAK, REMEMBERING THE THREAT OF THE GREAT KAHN, SHUDDERS WITH DREAD.

NO ENEMY OF THE HUN IS ON THAT PASS, FOR, LED BY HULTA DOWN A SECRET WAY, THEY HAVE DESCENDED TO THE PLAIN CLOSE BY THE FORTIFIED CAMP.

MIDNIGHT, AND A WEARY SUPPLY TRAIN ARRIVES AT THE GATE AND CLAMORS FOR ENTRANCE.

THE GATE SWINGS WIDE AND THROUGH THE GUARDS THE TIRED, TRAVEL-STAINED CARAVAN SLOWLY MAKES ITS WAY. THE GATES ARE SWINGING SHUT WHEN.......

.......VAL HAD REMEMBERED THE WOODEN HORSE OF TROY......THE SAME TRICK......UP FROM THE PACK-HORSES LEAP ARMED MEN.....A SHORT SHARP STRUGGLE.....AGAIN THE GATES SWING WIDE – AND.....

.....ACROSS THE MOONLIT PLAIN COMES THE SWELLING THUNDER OF GALLOPING HORSES AND THE MOUNTED "HUN-HUNTERS" BURST FURIOUSLY INTO THE SLEEPING CAMP, SHOUTING.

THE IRRESISTIBLE CHARGE OF THE HORSE-MEN SPREADS PANIC EVERYWHERE.....THEN COME THE GRIM, EFFICIENT FOOT SOLDIERS UNDER VONDERMAN AND THE CAMP IS WON.

STIRRUPS
SAVE THIS STAMP

"YOUR LIFE HAS BEEN SPARED THAT YOU MAY CARRY THIS MESSAGE TO KARNAK."

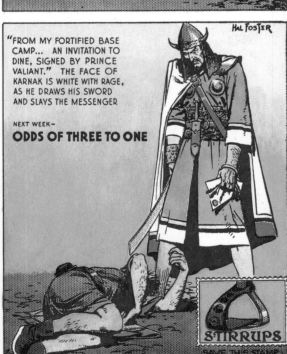

HAL FOSTER

"FROM MY FORTIFIED BASE CAMP... AN INVITATION TO DINE, SIGNED BY PRINCE VALIANT." THE FACE OF KARNAK IS WHITE WITH RAGE, AS HE DRAWS HIS SWORD AND SLAYS THE MESSENGER

NEXT WEEK–

ODDS OF THREE TO ONE

STIRRUPS
SAVE THIS STAMP

Synopsis: WHEN 'KARNAK, THE FEROCIOUS', LED HIS HUN ARMY AGAINST THE 'LEGION OF HUN-HUNTERS' THAT ELUSIVE BAND SLIPPED BEHIND HIM AND CAPTURED HIS FORTIFIED SUPPLY BASE, LEAVING HIS ARMY WITHOUT FOOD IN THE BARREN MOUNTAINS

THE CHEERY INVITATION FROM PRINCE VALIANT TO DINE IN HIS OWN CAMP IS AN INSULT THAT DRIVES KARNAK MAD WITH RAGE.

IT IS NOT LONG UNTIL THE WATCHERS ON THE PARAPET SEE THE VAST ARMY COME SWARMING DOWN THE PASS AND FORM ON THE PLAIN BEFORE THE CAMP

"TO YOUR STATIONS, COMRADES, THERE WILL BE A LIVELY PARTY ....THEY OUTNUMBER US THREE TO ONE..... GOOD LUCK ALL!"

KARNAK DRIVES HIS MEN MERCILESSLY... AGAIN AND AGAIN THEY STORM UP THE EARTHWORKS ONLY TO BE THROWN BACK. AT LAST NIGHT PUTS AN END TO THAT TERRIBLE DAY AND THE EXHAUSTED LIVING DROP TO REST BESIDE THE PEACEFUL DEAD.

1400
SAVE THIS STAMP

THE NEXT DAY IS QUIET – VICTORY HAD BEEN THEIRS, BUT NOT WITHOUT COST. THE SILENCE OF THE HUNS OUTSIDE IS LIKE AN UNSPOKEN THREAT.

»THE NEXT ATTACK WILL BE BY STARVING, DESPERATE MEN, MEN MAD WITH HUNGER...OUR DEFENDERS ARE TOO FEW TO GUARANTEE ANOTHER VICTORY...« VAL HESITATES, THEN, HIS FACE ALIGHT WITH ENTHUSIASM, HE UNFOLDS ANOTHER AUDACIOUS PLAN!

IN THE EARLY DAWN THE "HUN-HUNTERS" MARCH OUT AND FORM IN BATTLE ARRAY ....AND THE DESPAIRING KARNAK ROARS FOR JOY;- FOR YEARS HIS HUNS HAVE BEEN INVINCIBLE IN OPEN BATTLE!

NEXT WEEK- **VAL RETREATS. FOR A REASON!**

1918
SAVE THIS STAMP

Synopsis: AS USUAL, THE "LEGION OF HUN-HUNTERS" UNDER PRINCE VALIANT'S LEADERSHIP, HAS AVOIDED BATTLE WITH SUPERIOR FORCES AND STRUCK AT THE WEAKEST SPOT, THE SUPPLY BASE. "KARNAK, THE FEROCIOUS" IS PREPARING FOR AN ASSAULT WHEN THE "HUN-HUNTERS" ISSUE FORTH IN BATTLE FORMATION.

FOR THE FIRST TIME KARNAK BEHOLDS HIS ENEMY AND IS AMAZED TO SEE HOW FEW THEY ARE. THE HUNS FORM THEIR BATTLE-LINE AND BOTH SIDES CHARGE!

KARNAK SHOUTS FOR JOY, AS HIS INVINCIBLE HUNS SWEEP DOWN ON THE SCANTY, RAGGED LINE OF HUN-HUNTERS, MOST OF WHOM ARE UNMOUNTED!

AT THE FIRST SHOCK THE HUN-HUNTERS WHEEL THEIR HORSES AND FLY FROM THE FIELD IN PANIC......

AND THE HUNS, MOST FEROCIOUS WARRIORS THE WORLD HAS EVER SEEN, ARE UNLEASHED IN A SCREAMING MOB UPON THE FLEEING ENEMY!

SUDDENLY, THROUGH THE DUST OF THEIR RETREATING COMRADES, APPEAR THE FORGOTTEN FOOT-SOLDIERS BEHIND A GLEAMING WALL OF SPEARS AND SHARPENED STAKES AND THE FRONT LINE OF HUNS GOES DOWN BEFORE A HISSING CLOUD OF ARROWS!

FOR A MOMENT THE WILD RUSH IS HALTED, CONFUSED;— THEN, FROM A HIDDEN GULLEY COMES THE FULL FORCE OF VAL'S MOUNTED TROOPS AT A GALLOP.

NOTE:— IT IS A CURIOUS FACT THAT THE STRATEGY OF A KNIGHT OF KING ARTHUR'S ROUND TABLE, PRINCE VALIANT, SHOULD HAVE CAUSED THE DOWNFALL OF BRITAIN... FOR IN 1066, WILLIAM, THE CONQUEROR, USED THIS SAME PLAN AT THE BATTLE OF HASTINGS AND ALL ENGLAND FELL TO THE NORMANS.

PRINCE VALIANT'S STRATEGY IS SUCCESSFUL: THE HUN BATTLE FORMATION HAS BROKEN, THE FOOT SOLDIERS HAD MOMENTARILY CONFUSED THEM; THEN, INTO THE BEWILDERED MASS THE TERRIBLE, ARMORED WEDGE CLEAVES LIKE A PLOWSHARE!

NEXT WEEK— **MEDIEVAL PEACE TREATY!**

HAL FOSTER

Copr. 1940 King Features Syndicate, Inc. World rights reserved

158
2-18

Prince Valiant

IN THE DAYS OF KING ARTHUR
BY Harold R Foster

Synopsis: VICTORY! THE CONFUSED AND BROKEN RANKS OF THE HUN ARMY HAVE FLED WILDLY WITH THE GRIM VICTORS IN MERCILESS PURSUIT. PRINCE VALIANT WATCHES WEARILY; HIS PART IS ACCOMPLISHED; HE HAS SHOWN THE WORLD THAT THE HUN IS NOT INVINCIBLE.

THE STRATEGY, THE CRASH OF BATTLE, A BRAVE HARD-FIGHTING ENEMY AND THEN VICTORY; THESE THINGS ARE THE BREATH OF LIFE TO A WARRIOR! BUT VAL SICKENS AT THE TERRIBLE SLAUGHTER THAT FOLLOWS THESE MEDIEVAL BATTLES

AS HE RIDES SLOWLY BACK TO CAMP HE HEARS A SMALL VOICE CALLING HIM. HE HALTS AND THERE, PINNED TO A SADDLE WITH A CRUEL, BARBED ARROW, IS HULTA, THE MESSENGER.

GENTLY HE WORKS THE ARROW LOOSE FROM THE SADDLE. HULTA SWOONS.

TAKING THE SLENDER FIGURE IN HIS ARMS VAL REPROACHES HIMSELF: *"TO THINK I HAVE SENT HIM WITH MESSAGES TO MY OFFICERS IN THE THICK OF EVERY FIGHT AND HE IS ONLY A BOY!"*

THE WOUND IS NOT SERIOUS; VAL CUTS THE UGLY BARBED HEAD FROM THE ARROW AND WITHDRAWS THE SHAFT.

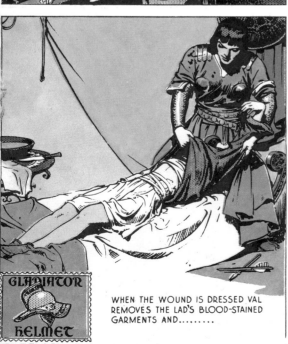

WHEN THE WOUND IS DRESSED VAL REMOVES THE LAD'S BLOOD-STAINED GARMENTS AND.........

GREAT GLEAMING COILS OF COPPER-COLORED HAIR SPREAD SLOWLY OVER THE PILLOW LIKE BRIGHT SERPENTS .... HULTA IS A GIRL!

NEXT WEEK— **A GIRL AND A PROPHECY!**

159 2-25-40 Copr. 1940, King Features Syndicate, Inc., World rights reserved

Hal FOSTER

MYSTERIOUS DEATH OF ATTILA — SAVE THIS STAMP

Prince Valiant

IN THE DAYS OF KING ARTHUR
BY
Harold R Foster

Registered U.S. Patent Office.

HUNS GATHER IN HUNGARY — SAVE THIS STAMP

Synopsis: BACK FROM THE VICTORIOUS BATTLE-FIELD COMES PRINCE VALIANT, CARRYING IN HIS ARMS THE LIMP FORM OF HULTA PIERCED THROUGH BY AN ENEMY ARROW. AND HULTA, WHO HAS CARRIED MESSAGES SAFELY THROUGH THE DANGER AND TURMOIL OF BATTLE, TURNS OUT TO BE A GIRL!

"SO YOU HAVE FOUND ME OUT, MY PRINCE?" "YES," SAYS VAL, "AND WHEN THE MEN KNOW THERE IS A YOUNG GIRL IN CAMP THERE WILL BE TROUBLE. WHY DID YOU MASQUERADE AS A BOY?"

" MY FATHER WAS A CHIEFTAIN OF THE SHEPHERD TRIBES HEREABOUT. THE HUNS CAME.....ONLY I ESCAPED. EVEN WOMEN MUST FIGHT NOW-A-DAYS AND I AM A WARRIOR'S DAUGHTER.

"...... AND ANOTHER WORRY FOR ME", ADDS VAL. "OH! WELL, I'LL EVEN MATTERS UP BY PASSING ON A WORRY TO KALLA KHAN." AND HE SENDS FOR TWO HUN PRISONERS AND THE BODY OF "KARNAK, THE FEROCIOUS".

AND KALLA KHAN IS NOT OVERLY PLEASED WITH THE GHASTLY PRESENT NOR THE MESSAGE WHICH READS, "YOU PROMISED TO CUT OFF THE HEAD OF 'KARNAK, THE FEROCIOUS' SHOULD HE FAIL. I HAVE COURTEOUSLY SAVED YOU THIS TROUBLE; IT WAS A PLEASURE. MANY MORE OF YOUR GENERALS WILL FAIL AND ADD THEIR HEADS TO YOUR COLLECTION FOR I HAVE SHOWN THE WORLD THE HUNS ARE NOT INVINCIBLE. THE HUNS ALSO KNOW THIS AND THEIR POWER IS GONE FOREVER." AND IN HIS HEART KALLA KHAN KNOWS THIS TO BE TRUE.

HAL FOSTER

"DELIVER THIS MESSAGE AND THIS CASKET TO KALLA KHAN OF THE HUNS AND", HE ADDS OMINOUSLY, "IT IS BETTER NOT TO FAIL."

INVADER ENGLAND 460 A.D. HORSA SAXON — SAVE THIS STAMP

WILLIAM A.D. 1066 THE CONQUERER — SAVE THIS STAMP

NEXT WEEK – GIRL TROUBLE.

Synopsis: CALLING HIS COUNCIL TOGETHER, PRINCE VALIANT SPEAKS AS FOLLOWS: *FOR ME THIS WAR AND ITS CARES AND WORRIES ARE ENDED. YOU, PISCARO, HUNT DOWN ALL THE REMAINING HUNS WITHOUT MERCY; VONDERMAN, FORTIFY THE PASS. TRISTRAM, ESTABLISH A FORM OF GOVERNMENT; DE GATIN, DIVIDE THE LAND AMONG THE WARRIORS. SLITH, YOU DIVIDE THE LOOT ACCORDING TO RANK. AND YOU, GAWAIN, MY OLD MASTER, PLEASE STAY OUT OF TROUBLE FOR YET A LITTLE WHILE!*

"AND HULTA, IT SEEMS, IS A GIRL. SHE IS UNDER MY PROTECTION; WHO HARMS HER MUST ANSWER TO ME."

HULTA, GRACEFUL AND HEALTHY AS A YOUNG ANIMAL, SOON RECOVERS FROM HER WOUND. EVERYONE AGREES THAT SHE GIVES A DECORATIVE TOUCH TO THE CAMP.

NO ONE ADMIRES HER MORE THAN SLITH, WHO, REMEMBERING THAT HE HAD BEEN HER CHOSEN FRIEND WHEN SHE WAS MASQUERADING AS A BOY, THINKS...... WELL......

KNOWING SHE IS ALONE IN HER TENT HE MAKES BOLD TO ENTER......

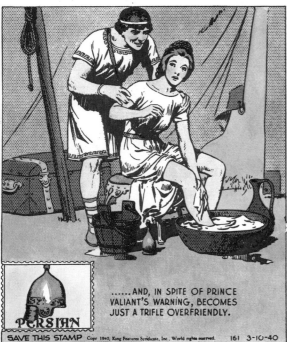

......AND, IN SPITE OF PRINCE VALIANT'S WARNING, BECOMES JUST A TRIFLE OVERFRIENDLY.

PERSIAN — SAVE THIS STAMP — Copr 1940, King Features Syndicate, Inc., World rights reserved. 161 3-10-40

HEARING A CRASH AND A YELL FROM HULTA'S TENT VAL RUNS TO INVESTIGATE AND FINDS THE GIRL WEEPING OVER THE UNCONSCIOUS SLITH! "OH! I HAVE HURT THE POOR BOY!"

HAL FOSTER

"I'VE LOVED THIS POOR, SHREWD LITTLE GREEK CLOWN FROM THE FIRST", SHE EXPLAINS, "I JUST CAN'T HELP IT!"

NEXT WEEK—
A KINGDOM IS FOUNDED.

BABYLONIAN — SAVE THIS STAMP

Synopsis: SLITH, ONE-TIME THIEF, IS A VERY CLEVER LAD; IN FACT, TOO CLEVER FOR HIS OWN GOOD, AND WHEN HULTA TURNS OUT TO BE NOT AN AGILE BOY, BUT A SPLENDID TALL GIRL, SHE HAS TO BREAK AN OAKEN WATER BUCKET ON HIS HEAD IN ORDER TO TEACH HIM RESPECT FOR A HELPLESS MAID!

"SO, HULTA, YOU LOVE THE LITTLE RASCAL? I DON'T SEE HOW HE CAN LONG WITHSTAND THE ARDOR OF YOUR WOOING," LAUGHS VAL.

BESIDE A COOL SPRING SLITH BATHES HIS BATTERED BROW. HIS RESPECT FOR HULTA IS AS GREAT AS THE ACHE IN HIS HEAD, WHICH IS CONSIDERABLE. A WARRIOR'S DAUGHTER, HE REFLECTS, IS TOO HIGH-SPIRITED FOR HIM!

WHILE THE WARRIOR'S DAUGHTER WEEPS LIKE ANY OTHER YOUNG GIRL, THINKING SHE HAS SLAIN CUPID WITH A WATER BUCKET.

MEANWHILE, A PROBLEM CONFRONTS THE COUNCIL. A LARGE TERRITORY HAS BEEN RE-CAPTURED, FORTIFIED AND A SYSTEM OF GOVERNMENT INSTALLED, BUT NO RULER CAN BE FOUND. WITH THE WAR AT AN END ALL THE OFFICERS LONG FOR THEIR DISTANT HOMES AGAIN. QUIETLY HULTA LEAVES THE COUNCIL

WITHIN HER TENT SHE UNPACKS THE GREAT SWORD AND SHIELD HER FATHER HAD CARRIED WHEN, IN HAPPIER TIMES, HE HAD RULED THE SHEPHERD TRIBES HEREABOUTS

LILY OF FRANCE — SAVE THIS STAMP

SLOWLY SHE WALKS THROUGH THE CAMP CHANTING AN ANCIENT BATTLE HYMN AND THE WARRIORS OF HER TRIBE, RECOGNIZING THEIR CHIEFTAIN'S DAUGHTER, FOLLOW

162. 3.17.40.

BEFORE THE COUNCIL PAVILION SHE HALTS "MY FATHER RULED ALL THESE LANDS BEFORE THE COMING OF THE HUNS - I AM HIS DAUGHTER. CAN YOU FIND A BETTER RULER?"

HAL FOSTER

— A Rival !

Copr 1940. King Features Syndicate, Inc., World rights reserved

GOLDEN EAGLE OF ROME — SAVE THIS STAMP

RED STALLION OF TRULE
SAVE THIS STAMP

Prince Valiant

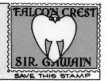
FALCON CREST
SIR GAWAIN
SAVE THIS STAMP

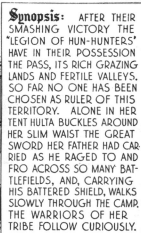

Synopsis: AFTER THEIR SMASHING VICTORY THE "LEGION OF HUN-HUNTERS" HAVE IN THEIR POSSESSION THE PASS, ITS RICH GRAZING LANDS AND FERTILE VALLEYS. SO FAR NO ONE HAS BEEN CHOSEN AS RULER OF THIS TERRITORY. ALONE IN HER TENT HULTA BUCKLES AROUND HER SLIM WAIST THE GREAT SWORD HER FATHER HAD CARRIED AS HE RAGED TO AND FRO ACROSS SO MANY BATTLEFIELDS, AND, CARRYING HIS BATTERED SHIELD, WALKS SLOWLY THROUGH THE CAMP. THE WARRIORS OF HER TRIBE FOLLOW CURIOUSLY.

" MY FATHER RULED ALL THE LANDS HEREABOUT BEFORE THE COMING OF THE HUN.....THESE ARE WARRIORS WHO HAVE FOLLOWED THIS SWORD AND THIS SHIELD.......THEY WILL STILL FOLLOW THEM. I WILL RULE THE LAND!"

FOR A LONG MOMENT VAL GAZES INTO THE CALM, FEARLESS EYES OF THIS TALL GIRL. "BY THE GODS I BELIEVE·YOU ARE THE ONE TO DO IT!" HE EXCLAIMS.

"WHAT IS THE CAUSE OF ALL THIS MISERY, SLITH?"
"HULTA.....SHE IS A GODDESS, NEVER HAVE I KNOWN A LOVELIER GIRL, BUT, ALAS! SHE IS TOO FAR ABOVE ME NOW!"
"I HAVE REASON TO BELIEVE SHE WILL LISTEN TO WHATEVER YOU MAY HAVE TO SAY." HINTS VAL.

HOPEFULLY, SLITH GOES IN SEARCH OF HULTA AND FINDS HER RETURNING FROM A BEAR HUNT.

"STAY A WHILE, HULTA, THERE IS SOMETHING I MUST TELL YOU AND A QUESTION I MUST ASK."

MODERN
BOXING-GLOVE
SAVE THIS STAMP

LEAPING LIGHTLY DOWN FROM THE HALF-WILD STALLION SHE HAS BEEN RIDING AND SENDING THE HARD-RIDING ESCORT ON WITH THE BEAR SHE HAS JUST SLAIN, HULTA TIMIDLY SAYS "YES" TO SLITH'S QUESTION.
163 3-24.40.

JOYOUSLY THE TWO LOVERS RIDE BACK TO CAMP; FOR SLITH TRULY LOVES THIS SPLENDID GIRL NOW THAT SHE IS CHIEFTAIN OF A RICH LAND AND IS VERY, VERY WEALTHY!

Copr. 1940, King Features Syndicate, Inc., World rights reserved

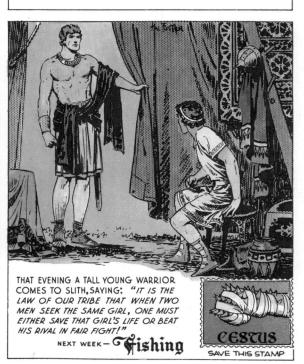

THAT EVENING A TALL YOUNG WARRIOR COMES TO SLITH, SAYING: "IT IS THE LAW OF OUR TRIBE THAT WHEN TWO MEN SEEK THE SAME GIRL, ONE MUST EITHER SAVE THAT GIRL'S LIFE OR BEAT HIS RIVAL IN FAIR FIGHT!"
NEXT WEEK— **Fishing**

CESTUS
SAVE THIS STAMP

"LIBERATOR"
SAVE THIS STAMP

Prince Valiant
IN THE DAYS OF KING ARTHUR
BY HAROLD R FOSTER

"LIBERATOR"
SAVE THIS STAMP

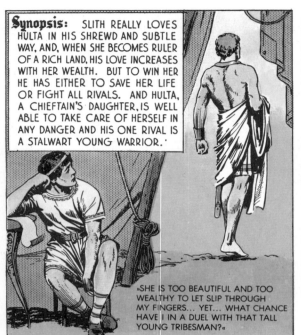

Synopsis: SLITH REALLY LOVES HULTA IN HIS SHREWD AND SUBTLE WAY, AND, WHEN SHE BECOMES RULER OF A RICH LAND, HIS LOVE INCREASES WITH HER WEALTH. BUT TO WIN HER HE HAS EITHER TO SAVE HER LIFE OR FIGHT ALL RIVALS. AND HULTA, A CHIEFTAIN'S DAUGHTER, IS WELL ABLE TO TAKE CARE OF HERSELF IN ANY DANGER AND HIS ONE RIVAL IS A STALWART YOUNG WARRIOR.

»SHE IS TOO BEAUTIFUL AND TOO WEALTHY TO LET SLIP THROUGH MY FINGERS... YET... WHAT CHANCE HAVE I IN A DUEL WITH THAT TALL YOUNG TRIBESMAN?«

FEELING THE NEED OF ADVICE, SYMPATHY AND HELP HE GOES TO PRINCE VALIANT'S TENT ONLY TO FIND, THAT VAL HAD LEFT CAMP AT DAWN, ALONE.

FOR DAYS HE HAD BEEN BUSY WITH LANCEWOOD AND THREAD, COLORED FEATHERS, GLUE, HOOKS, HORSEHAIR AND LINE. · NOW HE IS OFF TO THE CLEAR MOUNTAIN STREAMS FOR A FEW DAYS SPORT.

FOR VAL GREW UP IN SPORT-LOVING ENGLAND AND A FEW DAYS ON THE TROUT STREAMS BACK AMONG THE HILLS IS NOT TO BE MISSED.

DEEP IN THE FOREST VAL LETS THE LONELY MUSIC OF WIND IN THE TREE-TOPS AND THE MERRY SONG OF RUNNING WATER SOOTHE AWAY THE CARES AND ANX-IETIES OF HIS GREAT CAMPAIGN.

BUT THE STORY OF THAT VICTORY SPREAD FAR AND WIDE AND KINGS AND RULERS ALL ACROSS THE LAND SEND ENVOYS, EACH BEARING THE SAME MESSAGE.

MOHAMMEDANS
TAKE AFRICA 704 A.D.
SAVE THIS STAMP

DURING VAL'S ABSENCE THEY COME, AND RICH AND MAGNIFICENT ARE THESE NOBLE EMISSARIES WITH THEIR GLIT-TERING RETINUES.

HAL FOSTER

Copr. 1940, King Features Syndicate, Inc., World rights reserved.
164 3-31-40

"OUR ROYAL MASTERS HAVE SENT US TO OFFER YOUR ABSENT LEADER OUR WEALTH, OUR ARMIES, OUR LIVES. IF HE WILL LEAD US INTO PANNONIA AND ONCE AND FOR ALL CRUSH THE HUN NATION...... ONLY PRINCE VALIANT CAN DO THIS SUCCESSFULLY!"

NEXT WEEK—
The Answer

MOHAMMEDANS
TAKE SPAIN 714 A.D.
SAVE THIS STAMP

GALAHAD
SAVE THIS STAMP

Prince Valiant

IN THE DAYS OF
KING ARTHUR
BY
HAROLD R FOSTER

Registered U. S. Patent Office.

SAW
THE
HOLY
GRAIL
PERCIVAL
SAVE THIS STAMP

Synopsis: NEWS OF PRINCE VALIANT'S SUCCESSFUL CAMPAIGN AGAINST THE HUNS SPREAD QUICKLY AND FROM FAR AND WIDE COME THE ENVOYS OF KINGS OFFERING THEIR ARMIES FOR THE YOUNG PRINCE TO LEAD IN A WAR OF EXTERMINATION AGAINST THE HATED HUNS.

"THE MIGHTY PRINCE VALIANT WILL LEAD US ACROSS PANNONIA THROUGH A SEA OF HUNNISH BLOOD.... LIKE ALEXANDER, THE GREAT, HE INSPIRES A CERTAINTY OF VICTORY.... HIS BRILLIANT TACTICS RIVAL THE GREAT CAESAR, HIMSELF......"

"PARDON, SIR, BUT HERE COMES OUR MIGHTY CHIEFTAIN NOW!"   AND ENTERS, NOT A STERN GENERAL IN SHINING ARMOR, BUT A DISHEVELED, SUN-BRONZED LAD CARRYING A STRING OF FISH.

THE DIGNIFIED AMBASSADORS FROWN ANGRILY, FOR THEY THINK THIS AN ILL-TIMED JOKE.

MOORS INVADE
EUROPE 731
SAVE THIS STAMP

BUT WHEN THE LAD SPEAKS IT IS WITH THE CONFIDENCE AND COURTESY THAT BEFIT A PRINCE. "NOW, GENTLEMEN, I KNOW YOUR MISSION.... I ALSO KNOW THAT WARS OF AGGRESSION ARE BUT BREEDERS OF FUTURE WARS."

"HERE, UNDER MY HAND, IS THE HISTORY OF THE WORLD. NOWHERE CAN I FIND A LASTING CONQUEST BY FORCE. ALEXANDER AND CAESAR IN TURN CONQUERED THE WORLD BUT WHERE ARE THEIR CONQUESTS NOW?   WHAT OF BABYLON, OF PERSIA, OF CARTHAGE?   THE FRUITS OF CONQUEST ARE BUT SULLEN ENMITIES.   NO, NOBLE SIRS, I HAVE PLEDGED MY SWORD IN THE CAUSE OF JUSTICE AND FREEDOM ONLY!"

NEXT WEEK—
Slith's Cowardice.

CHARLES MARTEL
DEFEATS MOORS 732
SAVE THIS STAMP

165 4-7-40

Copr. 1940, King Features Syndicate, Inc., World rights reserved.

Synopsis: PRINCE VALIANT DECLINES TO ACCEPT THE COMMAND OF AN ARMY TO LEAD AGAINST THE DISORGANIZED HUNS. *"YOUR KINGDOMS WILL BE SAFE FROM HUN INVASIONS SO LONG AS THIS PASS IS HELD AGAINST THEM.— GIVE ITS DEFENDERS GENEROUS ASSISTANCE FOR YOUR OWN SAKES."*

"THIS IS HULTA, CHIEFTAINESS OF THE DEFENDERS OF THE PASS."

HULTA ESCORTS THE AMBASSADORS OVER THE PASS WHERE A STRONGLY FORTIFIED CITY IS RAPIDLY TAKING FORM.

THEN COMES THE TASK OF ESTABLISHING THE BORDERS AND ALLOTTING THE LAND. HAPPY DAYS FOR SLITH, FOR HE AND HULTA ARE MUCH TOGETHER.

HIS HAPPINESS WOULD BE COMPLETE WERE IT NOT FOR THAT TRIBAL CUSTOM; THAT HE MUST FIGHT ALL RIVALS TO PROVE HIMSELF WORTHY

BANDS OF STARVING HUNS, FUGITIVES FROM THE DEFEATED ARMY, STILL INFEST THE HILLS.... SUCH A GANG HAS FOLLOWED THE PARTY FOR DAYS, SEEKING PLUNDER.

AT DAWN HULTA GOES TO BATHE IN A POOL FAR FROM THE CAMP. THE WATCHFUL HUNS CREEP CLOSER, GRINNING.

ABOVE THE MURMUR OF THE STREAM SLITH HEARS A MUFFLED SCREAM AND CRUEL LAUGHTER.

RUNNING SWIFTLY TOWARD THE SOUND, SLITH SEES HIS BELOVED HULTA STRUGGLING IN THE GRASP OF FIVE ARMED HUNS!

HAL FOSTER

SLITH PAUSES — HE LOVES THIS TAWNY GIRL, AND HER GREAT FORTUNE ALSO... BUT HE IS UNARMED, ONE AGAINST FIVE... ONE MUST BE LOGICAL ABOVE ALL ELSE, HE REFLECTS, STILL HESITATING...

NEXT WEEK— **Madness!**

166 4-14-40

Copr. 1940, King Features Syndicate, Inc., World rights reserved

DAGGER
SAVE THIS STAMP

Prince Valiant

Registered U. S. Patent Office.

IN THE DAYS OF
KING ARTHUR
BY
HAROLD R FOSTER

DAGGER
SAVE THIS STAMP

Synopsis: A BAND OF FUGITIVE HUNS COMES UPON HULTA BATHING SOME DISTANCE FROM THE CAMP. SLITH ARRIVES ON THE SCENE, UNARMED SAVE FOR HIS SLING AND SEES THE GIRL HE LOVES BEING TAKEN FROM HIM. LIFE IS SWEET, HE REFLECTS, EVEN WITHOUT HER AND HER GREAT WFAITH. WHY RISK IT?

HULTA FIGHTS BRAVELY, HOPELESSLY. HER BRUTAL CAPTORS LAUGH AS SHE GROWS WEAKER ...... THEN SOMETHING HAPPENS TO SLITH!......

...... HE GOES MAD, QUITE MAD! FORGOTTEN IS HIS SHREWDNESS, THE DANGER, THE ODDS AGAINST HIM....THE GIRL HE LOVES IS IN PERIL!

THEY SEE HIM COMING AND ONE GRINNING HUN PREPARES TO CUT DOWN THE RECKLESS, UNARMED FOOL.

BUT A SLING IS A TERRIBLE WEAPON IN THE HANDS OF AN EXPERT.......

.......AND EVEN IN HIS FRANTIC ANGER SLITH IS STILL AN EXPERT.

ANOTHER OF THE HUNS MAKES THE MISTAKE OF FORGETTING THEIR VICTIM IS A WARRIOR'S DAUGHTER.

CHARLEMAGNE
800 A.D.
EMPEROR OF ROME
SAVE THIS STAMP

AND AGAIN THE LOADED SLING DOES ITS WORK.

IT ALL HAPPENED SO QUICKLY THAT, BEFORE THE REMAINING HUNS CAN STRING THEIR BOWS, SLITH AND HULTA ARE RUNNING TOWARD THE RIVER.

167 4-21-40   Copr 1940, King Features Syndicate, Inc ; World rights reserved

AS THEY PLUNGE IN SLITH HEARS HULTA CRY...."I CAN'T SWIM!"

NEXT WEEK — **Targets!**

CHARLEMAGNE
DIED 814
SAVE THIS STAMP

VAL OF THE FENS — SAVE THIS STAMP

Prince Valiant

IN THE DAYS OF KING ARTHUR
BY HAROLD R. FOSTER

Registered U.S. Patent Office.

VAL THE SQUIRE — SAVE THIS STAMP

Synopsis: ALL HIS LIFE SLITH HAS LIVED BY SHREWDNESS AND CUNNING, BUT WHEN HULTA FALLS INTO THE CRUEL HANDS OF A BAND OF HUNS HE DOES A BRAVE, MAD, FOOLISH DEED.

THEY ARE INTO THE SWIRLING RIVER BEFORE SLITH REALIZES THAT HULTA CANNOT SWIM. NO TIME FOR GALLANTRY NOW, HE TAKES A FIRM GRASP ON HER LONG HAIR AND STRIKES OUT STRONGLY.

A ROCK IN MIDSTREAM OFFERS A TEMPORARY SHELTER FROM THE HISSING ARROWS.

THE SOUND OF SLITH'S SHOUTS COMES FAINTLY BACK TO CAMP.

JUST AS THE CLUTCHING WATERS DRAG THEM FROM THEIR HAVEN, HELP ARRIVES.

SWINGING DOWN WITH THE CURRENT SLITH REACHES SHORE WITH HIS FAIR BURDEN.

SUDDENLY HE REALIZES THAT THIS TAWNY GIRL IS MORE PRECIOUS TO HIM THAN LIFE ITSELF..... IT FRIGHTENS HIM A LITTLE.

TO THE TRIBESMEN HE CALMLY SAYS; "I INTEND TO MARRY YOUR CHIEFTAIN AND I AM READY TO FIGHT ALL RIVALS AS IS THE CUSTOM!"

SAVE THIS STAMP

"YOU HAVE FULFILLED THE LAW— YOU HAVE SAVED HER LIFE. LET ME BE THE FIRST TO HAIL OUR NEW CHIEF."

168 4-28-40 Copr. 1940, King Features Syndicate, Inc., World rights reserved

ALL THIS IS TOO MUCH FOR SLITH...... HE SITS DOWN. AS HE FEELS HER GENTLE ARMS AROUND HIM HE REFLECTS......"NOT ALL MY TRICKERY NOR ALL MY CLEVERNESS HAS BROUGHT ME SUCH SWEET REWARD AS THIS ONE DEED OF HEROISM!"

NEXT WEEK — **Farewell**

SAVE THIS STAMP

433 A.D.
THULE REGAINED
SAVE THIS STAMP

Prince Valiant

IN THE DAYS OF
KING ARTHUR
BY
HAROLD R FOSTER

Registered U. S. Patent Office.

ATTILA
THE WILD HUNS
RAVAGE EUROPE
SAVE THIS STAMP

Synopsis: AND SO CHANCE TAKES A HAND IN THE AFFAIRS OF SLITH AND HULTA AND CLEARS ALL OBSTACLES FROM THE PATH OF THEIR MARRIAGE. HEREAFTER SLITH IS TO SPEND HIS LIFE PLEASANTLY DELUDED INTO THE BELIEF THAT NOWHERE IN ALL THE WORLD IS THERE ANYONE HALF SO LOVELY AS HULTA.

AND HE WRITES VERY BAD POEMS TO HER BEAUTY AND SHE SINGS TO HIM LITTLE IDLE SONGS AND ALL THOSE WHO ARE ANNOYED BY THIS IMBECILITY REFLECT THAT MARRIAGE WILL SOON PUT AN END TO THEIR NONSENSE!

AWAY FROM HIS LOVED ONE SLITH IS PRACTICALLY SANE AND TAKES AN ACTIVE PART IN PLANNING THE DEFENSES OF THE PASS.

THE CAPTURED BASE-CAMP IS NOW ALMOST DESERTED. THE WARRIORS, MADE WEALTHY BY THEIR SHARE OF THE SPOILS OF WAR, HAVE GONE THEIR WAY, MOST OF THEM TO TAKE SERVICE UNDER SLITH AND HULTA AND JOIN THEIR TRIBE.

THEIR LAST BANQUET, IN HONOR OF THE MARRIAGE OF SLITH AND HULTA, IS A GAY AFFAIR WITH MUCH SONG AND JEST, LAUGHTER AND SUDDEN SILENCES. FOR THERE ARE HEAVY HEARTS BENEATH ALL THE GAIETY. OLD FRIENDS ARE PARTING AND THEY REMEMBER SHARED DANGERS AND SPLENDID DEEDS IN THE TIME THEY FOUGHT SO DESPERATELY TOGETHER. THE HOUR OF PARTING IS LIKE AN APPROACHING CLOUD.

BUT THE THREE KNIGHTS OF KING ARTHUR'S ROUND TABLE CANNOT BEAR TO PART FOR YET A LITTLE WHILE. THEY SET OUT FOR THE ETERNAL CITY, ROME.

Copr. 1940, King Features Syndicate, Inc., World rights reserved.

HAL FOSTER

BUT FATE HAS PLACED IN THEIR PATH CERTAIN GAMBLERS, A HATCHET AND A GIANT. THERE WILL BE DELAYS.

NEXT WEEK— **The Gamblers**

169 5-5-40

ARCHBISHOP CANTERBURY SAVE THIS STAMP

Prince Valiant

IN THE DAYS OF KING ARTHUR
BY
HAROLD R FOSTER

Registered U. S. Patent Office.

BRASTIUS SAVE THIS STAMP

Synopsis: PRINCE VALIANT HAS DONE MORE THAN SHATTER ONE HUN ARMY.... HE HAS DESTROYED THE CONFIDENCE OF A WHOLE NATION IN THEIR INVINCIBILITY. THEY BECOME NOTHING MORE THAN PETTY RAIDERS. NOW, THEIR WORK DONE, TRISTRAN, PRINCE VALIANT AND SIR GAWAIN SET OUT FOR ROME.

AT SUNSET THEY COME TO A SNUG VILLAGE......

AND STOP FOR THE NIGHT AT THE TAVERN.

THERE ARE THREE OTHER GUESTS, GAY YOUNG NOBLES WHO WHILE AWAY THE EVENING HOURS AT DICE. AS THE GAME PROGRESSES THE STAKES BECOME HIGHER...

..... AND SIR GAWAIN, EVER HUNGRY FOR EXCITEMENT JOINS THE GAMESTERS AND THE PLAY THEN BECOMES EARNEST.

DURING THE TIME THEY HAD WANDERED TOGETHER SLITH HAD SHOWN VAL MANY OF HIS SLY TRICKS, SOME OF WHICH, HE NOTICES, ARE USED BY THE BOGUS NOBLES AT THE GAMING TABLE.

BEFORE RETIRING FOR THE NIGHT VAL INSTRUCTS THE STABLE BOY TO CALL HIM IF THE THREE GAMBLERS SHOULD CALL FOR THEIR HORSES.

IN THE EARLY DAWN THE BOY WHISPERS, "THEY HAVE ORDERED THEIR HORSES SADDLED, SIR, AND WILL LEAVE IN A FEW MINUTES!"......

.FOR THE GAME HAS ENDED AND SIR GAWAIN IS ADDRESSING SIR GAWAIN "YOU ARE SIR, WITH MY COMPLIMENTS, A FOOL. I SUSPECT YOU OF BEING TOO STUPID TO LEARN A LESSON. LOSING ALL YOUR MONEY WAS BAD BUT STAKING YOUR HORSE AND GEAR WAS SHEER IDIOCY. I LOOK TO YOUR FUTURE WITH GRAVE MISGIVING!"

170 5-12-40

THERE IS AN OMINOUS FOREBODING ABOUT THE TWO MAILED FIGURES WHO SILENTLY BAR THE GAMBLERS' DEPARTURE.

NEXT WEEK **Gawain Turns Turtle.**

HAL FOSTER

GENSERIC · 455 A.D. · VANDAL KING · SAVE THIS STAMP

Prince Valiant

IN THE DAYS OF KING ARTHUR
BY HAROLD R. FOSTER

Registered U. S. Patent Office.

EMPEROR OF ROME · 453 A.D. · VALENTINIAN · SAVE THIS STAMP

Synopsis: THE THREE KNIGHTS OF THE ROUND TABLE, TRISTRAM, PRINCE VALIANT AND GAWAIN, STOP FOR THE NIGHT AT A TAVERN WHERE THREE GAMBLERS, MASQUERADING AS NOBLEMEN, ENTICE SIR GAWAIN INTO A GAME OF CHANCE AND FLEECE HIM.

WITHOUT A WORD BEING SPOKEN TRISTRAM AND VAL PROD THE BOGUS NOBLES BACK TO THE INN YARD AND CALL SIR GAWAIN.

«GAWAIN, DEAR CHILD, COME... SEE ME WIN BACK YOUR LOSSES. YOU ARE LUCKY THESE BAD MEN DIDN'T TAKE AWAY YOUR TOYS AND SWADDLING CLOTHES, TOO!»

"NOW, MY OILY FRIENDS, WAGER YOUR PURSES AGAINST MINE AND I WILL THROW YOUR DICE AS MY TRICKY FRIEND, SLITH, ONCE SHOWED ME....AND AS YOU DID LAST NIGHT. BEHOLD! I WIN!"

"THE CHEATS!" ROARS THE ANGRY GAWAIN. "I'LL HAVE THEIR HEARTS' BLOOD FOR THAT!" AND STEPS BACK TO WHIP OUT HIS SWORD.........

HE SAID LATER THAT NEVER AGAIN WOULD HE DRAW HIS SWORD IN AN INN YARD ON WASH-DAY!

INTO THE WASH-TUB HE PLUNGES, BRINGING THE CLOTHES-LINE DOWN IN HIS FALL!

CALLING THE INNKEEPER'S WIFE, VAL POINTS TO THE TANGLED HEAP, "I FEAR SOME ONE IS STEALING YOUR WASH!"

«OH! YOU THIEF! (THUMP), YOU VARLET! (WHACK) YOU MISCREANT! (BANG) GET OUT OF MY WASHTUB!»

171 5-19-40   Copr. 1940, King Features Syndicate, Inc., World rights reserved.

BUT NOBLE SIR GAWAIN, MUCH AS HE WISHES, CANNOT GET OUT OF THE TUB.   UNLESS HE RECEIVES HELP HE IS DOOMED TO WADDLE AROUND LIKE A TURTLE FOR THE REST OF HIS LIFE!

HAL FOSTER

NEXT WEEK— **Wounded Pride**

Prince Valiant

IN THE DAYS OF
KING ARTHUR
BY
HAROLD R FOSTER

Registered U. S. Patent Office.

KING BAN
OF BENWICK
SAVE THIS STAMP

KING BANS
GREAT
FOE
CLAUDAS
SAVE THIS STAMP

Synopsis: WHEN SIR GAWAIN FINDS HE HAS BEEN CHEATED AT DICE BY THREE GAMBLERS HE FLIES INTO A RAGE AND WHIPS OUT HIS SWORD.....UNFORTUNATELY HE BECOMES ENTANGLED IN A CLOTHES-LINE AND A WASH-TUB. FOR SO NOBLE A KNIGHT HIS SITUATION IS MOST UNDIGNIFIED!

"VAL, TRISTRAM, HELP ME ELSE I FINISH MY STAY ON EARTH, AMBLING ABOUT LIKE A CONFOUNDED TURTLE!"

IT IS THE HALF-WITTED STABLE BOY WHO FINALLY SOLVES THE PROBLEM WITH THE SUGGESTION THAT THEY CUT THE HOOPS AND BRINGS FORWARD A SHARP HATCHET.

BUT THE BOY SADLY MISJUDGES' THE FORCE NECESSARY TO CUT ONLY THE HOOP!

SOME INVALIDS GET SYMPATHY, BUT THE NATURE OF GAWAIN'S MISFORTUNE BRINGS FORTH ONLY JOKES AND LAUGHTER FROM HIS FRIENDS AND SCOWLS FROM HIM.

IT WILL BE TWO OR THREE DAYS BEFORE GAWAIN CAN RIDE AGAIN. HE GROANS AT THE ENFORCED IDLENESS.

MEANWHILE, TRISTRAM HAS TAKEN THE THREE GAMBLERS INTO THE INN YARD. 'IT IS THE CUSTOM OF ALL KNIGHTS TO DO SOME *USEFUL DEED EACH DAY,*« HE EXPLAINS, «*NOW, I WILL SHARPEN THIS LONG SWORD OF MINE, AND YOU...?*« THEY EYE THE GLEAMING SWORD DUBIOUSLY AND SET TO WORK

WHEN THEIR WORK IS FINISHED SIR TRISTRAM, WITH KNIGHTLY COURTESY, HELPS THEM ON THEIR WAY!

AS ALL TRUE KNIGHTS MUST PRACTISE CHIVALRY TO THE LADIES... TRISTRAM STOLLS TO THE SQUARE TO PRACTISE IT ON THE VILLAGE MAIDENS. THERE WERE NO COMPLAINTS.

172 5-26-40   Copr 1940, King Features Syndicate, Inc World rights reserved

HAL FOSTER

WHILE TO VAL, STROLLING IN THE OPPOSITE DIRECTION, COMES A BREATHLESS PEASANT... »*THE GIANT, THE GIANT COMES!*«

NEXT WEEK— **The Giant.**

THE LADY OF THE LAKE — SAVE THIS STAMP

Prince Valiant

IN THE DAYS OF
KING ARTHUR
BY
HAROLD R FOSTER

Registered U S Patent Office

LEODEGRANCE FATHER OF GUINEVERE — SAVE THIS STAMP

Synopsis: WHILE TRISTRAM, PRINCE VALIANT AND SIR GAWAIN ARE JOURNEYING TOWARD ROME THEY ARE DELAYED IN A MOUNTAIN VILLAGE WHILE GAWAIN RECOVERS FROM AN ACCIDENT. SUDDENLY A SHOUT GOES UP, *"THE GIANT, THE GIANT!"*

LOOKING UP THE ROAD, VAL SEES NO FEARSOME GIANT, BUT ONLY A POMPOUS LITTLE DWARF, WADDLING TOWARD THEM ON HIS SHORT, BOWED LEGS.

HALTING, THE DWARF FROWNS IMPORTANTLY AND READS FROM A LIST THE ARTICLES DEMANDED BY THE GIANT. *"SEND THESE ON TWO WORK-HORSES LED BY A MALE SLAVE OR MY TERRIBLE MASTER WILL COME IN ANGER!"*

"TWICE EACH YEAR," EXPLAINS THE VILLAGE CHIEF, *"THE GIANT MAKES DEMANDS ON ALL THE HAMLETS HEREABOUT..... MANY HAVE SOUGHT TO KILL HIM..... NONE HAVE RETURNED!"*

"I WILL BE THAT SLAVE AND I WILL RETURN... I HOPE!" SAYS VAL, THROWING A CLOAK OVER THE GREAT *"SINGING SWORD"*.

THE WAY LEADS OVER A BARREN WASTELAND, THEN DIPS INTO A NARROW GORGE. THE BATTERED SHIELDS AND HELMS OF DEFEATED KNIGHTS GIVE GRIM WARNING.

A WEIRD, SHADOWY PLACE OF FANTASTIC SHAPES AND BROODING SILENCE..... ALMOST ANYTHING IS MORE THAN LIKELY TO HAPPEN HERE..... VAL HAS THE STRANGE FEELING OF BEING WATCHED!

NEXT WEEK—
The Watcher.

Copr. 1940, King Features Syndicate, Inc., World rights reserved

173 6-2-40

THE DAME SLIGON — SAVE THIS STAMP

Prince Valiant

IN THE DAYS OF KING ARTHUR
BY
HAROLD R FOSTER

Registered U. S. Patent Office.

CLARIS — SAVE THIS STAMP

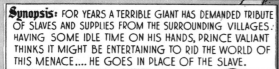

Synopsis: FOR YEARS A TERRIBLE GIANT HAS DEMANDED TRIBUTE OF SLAVES AND SUPPLIES FROM THE SURROUNDING VILLAGES. HAVING SOME IDLE TIME ON HIS HANDS, PRINCE VALIANT THINKS IT MIGHT BE ENTERTAINING TO RID THE WORLD OF THIS MENACE.... HE GOES IN PLACE OF THE SLAVE.

AS HE LEADS THE LADEN HORSES DOWN THE FEARFUL CHASM, HE FEELS AS THOUGH STRANGE EYES ARE WATCHING HIM.

HE STEALS A QUICK GLANCE BEHIND AND SEES THAT WHICH HE FEARS MOST TO FIND. AGAINST A FANTASTIC BACKGROUND IS A FANTASTIC MONSTER, HUGE AND MENACING.

VAL WALKS ON, WONDERING. HE MUST HAVE PASSED RIGHT BY THE MONSTER, YET HIS HORSES HAD SHOWN NO FEAR. TIMID, WILD CREATURES GAMBOL ABOUT THE GIANT'S FEET. THERE MUST BE SOME ANSWER.

THE CANYON NARROWS TO A MERE CRACK IN WHICH A STRONG GATE-WAY IS SET........THERE IS NO TURNING BACK NOW

PASSING THROUGH, VAL STEALS A BACKWARD GLANCE— THE GIANT IS LOCKING THE MASSIVE GATES....TRAPPED!

THE TRAIL DESCENDS INTO A GROVE OF TREES AND THERE VAL TAKES THE BOW AND ARROWS HE HAD CONCEALED AND DISAPPEARS AMONG THE FOLIAGE.

SOON THE HUGE CREATURE GOES STRIDING BY!

AT THE END OF THE WOODS HE DISCOVERS THE ABSENCE OF THE NEW SLAVE.....WHEELING ABOUT HE SHOUTS HOARSELY, *"YOU CANNOT ESCAPE, YOU MUST COME TO ME OR STARVE!"*

174 6-9-40

AS HE TURNS HOMEWARD, A YELPING PACK OF OUTCAST DOGS SURROUNDS HIM, LEAPING AND BARKING.

NEXT WEEK—

A Strange Household

Copr. 1940, King Features Syndicate, Inc., World rights reserved.

A TORMENTOR
SAVE THIS STAMP

Prince Valiant

IN THE DAYS OF KING ARTHUR
BY
HAROLD R FOSTER

A TORTURER
SAVE THIS STAMP

Synopsis: PRINCE VALIANT UNDERTAKES A QUEST TO RID THE COUNTRY-SIDE OF A TROUBLESOME GIANT. FAR OUT IN A BARREN WASTELAND IS A GREEN VALLEY, ITS ONLY ENTRANCE GUARDED BY A STRONG GATEWAY....THE WILY GIANT CLOSES THIS GATEWAY BEHIND THE PRINCE. FROM A TREE-TOP VAL WATCHES THE MONSTER STRIDING HOMEWARD WITH HIS YELPING DOGS.

LIKE A GOOD GENERAL VAL DECIDES TO PLAN A RETREAT BEFORE VENTURING ON AN ATTACK. THE STREAM THAT WATERS THIS RICH VALLEY MUST HAVE AN OUTLET......

......BUT THE OUTLET FALLS SHEER INTO A STILL LOWER CANYON.

NOR CAN HE SCALE THE WALLS.... BELOW HIM GRAZE FLOCKS OF SHEEP AND FAT CATTLE. SLAVES WORK IN THE SUNNY FIELDS.

AT SUNDOWN HE REPAIRS AGAIN TO THE WOOD AND THERE BUSIES HIMSELF UNTIL DARK.

SILENTLY, THROUGH THE VELVETY DARKNESS, VAL CREEPS TO THE GIANT'S HOUSE AND RAISES HIS CROOK TO THE TOP OF THE WALL.

ONCE ON THE WALL HE CAN REACH THE LEDGE OF A LIGHTED WINDOW. FROM WITHIN COMES A CONFUSED MEDLEY OF STRANGE VOICES.

VAL PEERS THROUGH THE SHUTTERS ON A NIGHTMARE SCENE.... AROUND THAT LITTERED BOARD ARE GATHERED THE DEFORMED, THE MISSHAPEN, THE CRIPPLED, THE HALF-WITTED, DWARF AND GIANT....THE WORLD'S OUTCASTS.

NEXT WEEK—
Prince Valiant meets the Giant.

Copr. 1940, King Features Syndicate, Inc., World rights reserved
175 6-16-40

Synopsis: PRINCE VALIANT HAS COME TO THIS HIDDEN VALLEY TO KILL A FEARSOME GIANT WHO HAS TERRORIZED THE COUNTRYSIDE FOR YEARS. VAL IS FRANKLY PUZZLED THAT SO DREAD A MONSTER SHOULD KEEP AND CARE FOR ALL THE OUTCASTS, WHETHER MAN OR BEAST

AT LAST VAL THINKS HE HAS THE ANSWER TO THE PUZZLE . . . IN THE MORNING HE WILL PUT IT TO THE TEST

SO AT SUN-UP HE TAKES HIS STAND IN FULL VIEW . . . HIS BOW AND QUIVER OF ARROWS CONCEALED BEHIND HIS CLOAK.

"SO," BELLOWS THE GIANT, "OUR NEW SLAVE HAS DECIDED TO WORK RATHER THAN STARVE."

SUDDENLY VAL WHIPS OUT HIS BOW. "MOVE BUT ONE MORE STEP," HE CRIES, "AND I'LL SHOOT EVERY DOG IN YOUR PACK !"

THE HEAVY, STUPID FACE OF THE GIANT LOSES ITS EVIL SCOWL; FOR A MOMENT HE SEEMS PUZZLED, THEN A LOOK OF SORROW COMES INTO HIS EYES. "NO, NO," HE CRIES, "DON'T HARM MY FRIENDS !"

"THEY ARE BUT POOR OUTCASTS FROM THE CRUELTY OF SUCH AS YOU. SPARE THEM AND YOU MAY GO FREE. I HAVE MADE THIS VALLEY A REFUGE FOR ALL WHO HAVE SUFFERED THE SNEERS AND ABUSE OF MEN. . . . GO, BUT KEEP OUR SECRET !"

NEXT WEEK-
The Life of a Giant.

Copr. 1940, King Features Syndicate, Inc., World rights reserved

176 6-23-40

DANE — SAVE THIS STAMP

Prince Valiant

IN THE DAYS OF KING ARTHUR
BY HAROLD R FOSTER

Registered U. S. Patent Office.

SOLDIER OF FAR CATHAY — SAVE THIS STAMP

Synopsis: PRINCE VALIANT SETS OUT TO KILL A TERRIBLE GIANT; INSTEAD HE HUMBLES THAT GIANT BY THREATENING TO KILL HIS BELOVED DOGS. THE GIANT TELLS HIS STORY

3. WHILE STILL A BOY I WAS SO HUGE THAT MY POOR PARENTS COULD NO LONGER FEED ME.

2. "AT FIRST I WAS LIKE ANY OTHER CHILD, BUT SOMETHING HAPPENED TO ME.... INSIDE. I STARTED TO GROW RAPIDLY.

4. I WAS LOOKED UPON AS SOMETHING QUEER, TO BE LAUGHED AT, ABUSED, THE BUTT OF ALL JOKES..... IT WAS CRUEL.

5. IN DESPERATION I LEFT MY VILLAGE, BUT STRANGERS LOOKED UPON ME WITH HORROR. IN THEIR FEAR THEY CALLED ME A MONSTER.

7. MANY KNIGHTS HAVE SOUGHT TO KILL ME, BUT I WIELD A MORE TERRIBLE WEAPON THAN ANY KNIGHT CAN CARRY.

HAL FOSTER

1.

6. I SOON LEARNED TO TAKE ADVANTAGE OF THEIR FEAR TO GET WHAT I NEEDED.

8. AT LAST I FOUND THIS VALLEY... SINCE THEN I HAVE MADE IT A HAVEN TO ALL WHO, LIKE ME, HAVE SUFFERED FROM MAN'S CRUELTY... THE MAIMED, THE TWISTED, THE DWARF, THE WITCH: ALL WHO ARE OUTCASTS."

NEXT WEEK: **The Giant's Victory**

177- 6-30-40   Copr. 1940, King Features Syndicate, Inc., World rights reserved.

Prince Valiant

IN THE DAYS OF KING ARTHUR
BY
HAROLD R. FOSTER

Registered U. S. Patent Office.

THE CROWN OF THULE — SAVE THIS STAMP

CHALICE OF THE KING — SAVE THIS STAMP

Synopsis: THE FEARSOME GIANT THAT PRINCE VALIANT SET OUT TO KILL TELLS THE STORY OF HIS LIFE, OF RIDICULE AND ABUSE IN CHILDHOOD; FEAR AND HATRED IN MANHOOD. AND HOW HE LEARNED TO USE THE FEAR HE INSPIRED, TO SUPPORT AND CARE FOR ALL WHO ARE MAIMED OR OUTCAST.

"AND NOW YOU HAVE LEARNED MY SECRET," SAYS THE GIANT SADLY. "PEOPLE WILL NO LONGER FEAR ME— MY FRIENDS WILL STARVE."

"I SYMPATHIZE WITH YOU. NEVER-THE-LESS, I'VE PLEDGED MY KNIGHTLY WORD TO RID THE COUNTRYSIDE OF YOUR MENACE AND I WILL KEEP MY VOW.....BUT, IN THIS MANNER....."

"LOOK, YOUR FIELDS ARE FERTILE; YOUR HERDS AND FLOCKS INCREASE; YOU HAVE WEALTH BEYOND YOUR NEEDS. SO OPEN YOUR GATES TO COMMERCE WITH YOUR NEIGHBORS. EXCHANGE THEIR FEAR FOR THEIR RESPECT!"

"TRUST! FRIENDLINESS! THINGS I'VE NEVER KNOWN....TO BE A RESPECTED LANDOWNER, TOO GOOD TO BE TRUE, BUT I'LL TRY IT!"

CALLING HIS SLAVES TOGETHER, THE GIANT ANNOUNCES, "I GIVE YOU ALL YOUR FREEDOM. ANY WHO WISHES TO REMAIN WILL BE PAID A FAIR WAGE, GOOD FOOD AND LODGINGS."

THE GATES ARE FLUNG WIDE AND ALL THE WORKERS RUSH OUT TO FREEDOM, SHOUTING JOYOUSLY!

"YOUR IDEA WAS TOO GOOD TO BE TRUE! LOOK, MY FIELDS AND FLOCKS ARE UNATTENDED. NOBODY WILL WILLINGLY WORK FOR ONE THEY FEAR!"

"A MAN NEVER VALUES WHAT HE HAS, ONLY THAT WHICH HE CANNOT HAVE. WHEN THEY HAVE ENJOYED THEIR NEW— FOUND LIBERTY THEY WILL REMEMBER YOUR FAIR TREATMENT. SEE! EVEN NOW, SOME ARE RETURNING......."

178 7-7-40   Copr. 1940, King Features Syndicate, Inc., World rights reserved.

MOUNTED ON A WORK HORSE, VAL RETURNS TO HIS FRIENDS. "THE UNHAPPY SLAVES OF YESTERDAY WILL BE CONTENTED WORKERS TO-MORROW, AND ONLY BECAUSE A DISTANT GATE IS NOW UNLATCHED. WHO WAS IT THAT SAID,'MONKEYS ARE THE CRAZIEST PEOPLE'?"

NEXT WEEK— **Target Practice.**

HAL FOSTER

Prince Valiant

IN THE DAYS OF KING ARTHUR.
BY HAROLD R. FOSTER

Registered U. S. Patent Office.

THE STEWARD OF PERILOUS GARDE — SAVE THIS STAMP

PERILOUS GARDE — SAVE THIS STAMP

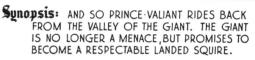

Synopsis: AND SO PRINCE VALIANT RIDES BACK FROM THE VALLEY OF THE GIANT. THE GIANT IS NO LONGER A MENACE, BUT PROMISES TO BECOME A RESPECTABLE LANDED SQUIRE.

"THE GIANT OFFERS GOOD WAGES FOR WORKERS ON HIS RICH ESTATE AND WILL TRADE IN CATTLE AND GRAIN WITH HIS NEIGHBORS. TREAT HIM WITH RESPECT AND YOU NEED NO LONGER FEAR HIM."

"THAT QUEST IS FINISHED. SO, MY COMRADES, IF GAWAIN'S DISTRESSING WOUND HAS HEALED WE CAN DEPART."

WITH MUCH GROANING SIR GAWAIN GETS PAINFULLY INTO HIS WELL-PADDED SADDLE AND THEY SET OUT ONCE MORE FOR ROME.

THEIR JOURNEY IS UNEVENTFUL UNTIL THE BLUE OF THE ADRIATIC SEA GLEAMS ON THE HORIZON. THEN THEY COME ACROSS A BAND OF TRAVELING MERCHANTS, HIDING BEHIND A LOW HILL.

"WE FEAR TO PROCEED, FOR YONDER SENTRY GIVES WARNING THAT RAIDING HUNS MUST BE CAMPED BELOW."

IT IS DEEMED ADVISABLE TO REMOVE THE SENTRY QUIETLY WITH AN ARROW, BUT THIS GIVES RISE TO AN ARGUMENT AS TO WHO IS BEST QUALIFIED FOR THE SHOT!

SO WAGERS ARE LAID, ARROWS CHOSEN WITH CARE AND, AT A GIVEN SIGNAL, THREE BOWS TWANG.

Copr. 1940, King Features Syndicate, Inc. World rights reserved

IT WAS RATHER TOUGH ON THE SENTRY BUT, AS TRISTRAM SAID AFTERWARD, HE WOULD HAVE DONE AS MUCH FOR US, IF HE HAD SEEN US FIRST.

IT IS JUST AS THE MERCHANTS SUSPECTED. BELOW THE SENTRY'S POST A BAND OF RAIDING HUNS IS ENCAMPED!

NEXT WEEK — **The Stampede.**

179 7-14-40

HAL FOSTER

179

412 A.D. ROMANS LEAVE BRITAIN — SAVE THIS STAMP

Prince Valiant

IN THE DAYS OF KING ARTHUR
BY HAROLD R. FOSTER

Registered U S Patent Office

KING ARTHUR 420 TO 460 A.D. — SAVE THIS STAMP

Synopsis: THE ROAD TO ROME WINDS DOWN FROM THE HILLS TO THE MARSHY PLAINS BORDERING THE ADRIATIC SEA AND THERE, BLOCKING THE PATH, IS AN ENCAMPMENT OF HUN RAIDERS.

THE BARBARIANS LOLL BY THE CAMPFIRES, WHILE THEIR HORSES GRAZE. AND ON A FAR RIDGE, SCOUTS ARE SPYING ON THEIR INTENDED VICTIMS, A GROUP OF WORKERS NEAR THE SEA.

ONE OF THE MERCHANTS IS DRESSED IN THE LATE SENTRY'S GARMENTS AND STANDS ON GUARD SO THE RAIDERS BELOW WILL NOT BECOME SUSPICIOUS.

"HUNS, HUNS, HUNS!" EXCLAIMS VAL TRAGICALLY. "MUST I SPEND ALL MY YOUNG LIFE FIGHTING HUNS? IS THERE NOTHING ELSE IN THIS WHOLE WIDE WORLD TO FIGHT?" "YOU MIGHT FIGHT YOUR TENDENCY TO LONG-WINDED DRAMATICS," SUGGESTS GAWAIN.

"NOW, VAL, HOW ABOUT A QUAINT AND AMUSING SCHEME TO LEND THE SPICE OF NOVELTY TO OUR COMING FUSS WITH THE ENEMY?"

"I HAVE IT! THE HUNS ARE RENOWNED HORSEMEN IT WOULD DISCOURAGE THEM GREATLY TO BE TRAMPLED TO DEATH BY THEIR OWN HORSES!"

SEVERAL OF THE MORE VENTURESOME OF THE MERCHANTS ARE GIVEN GREAT TORCHES AND MOUNTED ON PACK ANIMALS. BY A ROUND-ABOUT WAY THEY APPROACH THE RAIDERS' GRAZING MOUNTS.

WITH FLAMING TORCHES, WAVING CLOAKS AND SCREAMING LIKE DEMONS THEY CHARGE DOWN UPON THE STARTLED HERD.....AND THE STAMPEDE IS ON!

NEXT WEEK— *Venice is Born.*

HAL FOSTER

180 7-21-40   Copr 1940, King Features Syndicate, Inc World rights reserved

BATTERING RAM
SAVE THIS STAMP

Prince Valiant

Registered U S Patent Office

IN THE DAYS OF KING ARTHUR
BY
HAROLD R. FOSTER

SIEGE TOWER
SAVE THIS STAMP

Synopsis: THE ROAD TO ROME LEADS DOWN FROM THE SNOWY ALPS TO THE VENETIAN PLAINS AND THERE THE WAY IS BLOCKED BY THE CAMP OF A BAND OF HUNS. CLOSE TO THEM IN THE NARROW VALLEY GRAZE THE RAIDERS' HORSES. PRINCE VALIANT, TRISTRAM AND SIR GAWAIN MAKE QUICK PLANS TO WIN THROUGH.

HOWLING LIKE DEMONS AND WITH BLAZING TORCHES AND WAVING CLOAKS, THEY SWOOP DOWN UPON THE STARTLED MOUNTS... THE STAMPEDE IS ON! AND THE HUNS, MOST RENOWNED OF HORSEMEN, SUFFER THE IGNOMINY OF BEING TRAMPLED INTO THE DUST BY THEIR OWN STEEDS!

OUT ACROSS THE PLAIN THEY DRIVE THE HORSES WITH-OUT BOTHERING ABOUT THEIR BATTERED OWNERS, FOR THE HUN IS HELPLESS WHEN SET AFOOT.

SEVERAL MILES FARTHER ON THE THREE COMRADES MEET THE HUNS' IN-TENDED VICTIMS. *"WE ARE THE VENETI, HUNGARY IS ON OUR EAST-ERN BORDER AND THE HUNS HAVE DRIVEN US FROM OUR HOME-LAND TO SEEK SAFETY ON ISLANDS FAR OUT ON THE ADRIATIC SEA."*

"WE MUST HAVE STONE FOR BUILDING AND TIMBER FOR SHIPS, BUT THE HUNS HARRY OUR WORKMEN. WE CANNOT PREVAIL AGAINST THE BARBARIANS."

WHEN THE VENETI LEARN THAT THESE THREE KNIGHTS ARE THE FAMOUS LEADERS OF THE "HUN-HUNTERS" THEY PLEAD WITH THEM TO ORGANIZE AN ARMY OF DEFENSE.

WHILE SIR GAWAIN TURNS VENTURESOME YOUNG MEN INTO SWIFT, HARD-RIDING CAVALRY, PRINCE VALIANT TRAINS STEADY FOOT SOLDIERS IN THE METHODS HE FOUND SO SUCCESSFUL IN HIS RECENT CAMPAIGN AGAINST THEIR ENEMY.....

.....TRISTRAM PICKS THE BEST OF THE VENETI MANHOOD AND PATIENTLY, TIRELESSLY TRAINS THEM TO OFFICER THE TROOP.

THEN THEY GO HAPPILY ON THEIR WAY, RICHER NOW. BUT QUITE UNAWARE THAT THEY HAVE HELPED IN THE BUILDING OF VENICE.... VENICE, THE BEAUTIFUL, SOON TO RIVAL IN GRANDEUR AND POWER EVEN ROME, ITSELF!

NEXT WEEK- **Duck-Hunting.**

181 7-28-40

MOTHER OF ARTHUR
IGRAINE
SAVE THIS STAMP

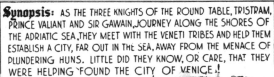
Prince Valiant

Registered U. S. Patent Office

IN THE DAYS OF
KING ARTHUR
BY
HAROLD R FOSTER

FATHER OF ARTHUR
UTHER PENDRAGON
SAVE THIS STAMP

Synopsis: AS THE THREE KNIGHTS OF THE ROUND TABLE, TRISTRAM, PRINCE VALIANT AND SIR GAWAIN, JOURNEY ALONG THE SHORES OF THE ADRIATIC SEA, THEY MEET WITH THE VENETI TRIBES AND HELP THEM ESTABLISH A CITY, FAR OUT IN THE SEA, AWAY FROM THE MENACE OF PLUNDERING HUNS. LITTLE DID THEY KNOW, OR CARE, THAT THEY WERE HELPING 'FOUND THE CITY OF VENICE.!

AT LAST THEY REACH PADOVA, THEIR FIRST GREAT ROMAN CITY; THE SQUALID POVERTY OF THE PRESENT LIVING AMID THE RUINED SPLENDOR OF THE PAST.

HERE THEY BUY SUPPLIES AND A RICH PAVILION; HIRE ATTENDANTS AND PROCEED ONWARD IN A STYLE MORE BEFITTING THEIR RANK. THE HEAVY TREAD OF INVADING ARMIES HAD LONG SINCE BROUGHT RUIN TO THE FAMED ROMAN ROADS.

IFAR OUT ON THE WIDE MARSHES OF THE PO THEY BEHOLD A STRANGE SIGHT.....WAVE AFTER WAVE OF WILDFOWL COME, WINGING OVER THE DISTANT ALPS TO CIRCLE AND GLIDE DOWN AMONG THE TALL REEDS.

TEAL AND WIDGEON, BRANT AND GEESE, SNIPE AND GOLDEN PLOVER....ALL THE FAMILIAR WATERFOWL OF DISTANT ENGLAND.... BRINGING RUMOR OF WINTRY STORMS IN THEIR MISTY NORTHERN HOMELAND.
THE PAVILION IS PITCHED 'AND THE THREE FRIENDS ABANDON THEMSELVES TO THE SPORT THEY USED TO ENJOY IN THE ENGLISH FENS.

LONG, HARD MONTHS OF FIGHTING LAY BEHIND THEM, ROME AND UNKNOWN ADVENTURES LIE AHEAD.... IN THE MEANTIME, THEY RELAX AND LET THE SUNNY, CAREFREE DAYS SLIP BY.

AT LAST THEY MOVE ON AGAIN, FOLLOWING THE RUINED ROAD UNTIL, IN THE DISTANCE, THEY BEHOLD THE WHITE TOWERS OF RAVENNA SHIMMERING IN THE SUNLIGHT....

.... IN THE SHADOW OF THE CITY'S GATE A SOMBER FIGURE IN ORIENTAL GARB AWAITS THEIR COMING.

NEXT WEEK— **The Oriental.**

182 8-4-40 Cope 1940, King Features Syndicate, Inc. World rights reserved

PISCARO
SAVE THIS STAMP

Prince Valiant

IN THE DAYS OF KING ARTHUR
BY
HAROLD R FOSTER

VAL'S DISGUISE
SAVE THIS STAMP

Synopsis: AFTER A WEEK OF HUNTING, THE THREE KNIGHTS OF THE ROUND TABLE RESUME THEIR LEISURELY JOURNEY TOWARD ROME. EVERYWHERE THEY ENCOUNTER RUIN AND DECAY. THE EMPIRE IS CRUMBLING. IN FACT, HERE AT RAVENNA, JUST TWENTY YEARS LATER, A WHITE-FACED BOY-EMPEROR WILL GIVE THE EMPIRE OVER TO THE BARBARIANS.

AS THEY ENTER THE CITY'S GATES, A STOOPED FIGURE IN ORIENTAL GARB APPRAISES THEM WITH KEEN EYES.

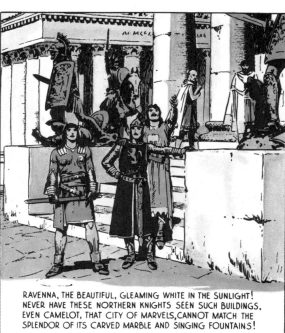

RAVENNA, THE BEAUTIFUL, GLEAMING WHITE IN THE SUNLIGHT! NEVER HAVE THESE NORTHERN KNIGHTS SEEN SUCH BUILDINGS, EVEN CAMELOT, THAT CITY OF MARVELS, CANNOT MATCH THE SPLENDOR OF ITS CARVED MARBLE AND SINGING FOUNTAINS!

FOR A WEEK THEY LINGER AMONG THE MANY WONDERS. THE WEALTH OF ITS LIBRARIES FASCINATES VAL.

AT NIGHT THEY REVEL IN THE LUXURY OF ROMAN ENTERTAINMENT

LIGHT-HEARTEDLY SIR GAWAIN SETS OUT TO LEARN THE LOCAL CUSTOMS AND DOES RIGHT WELL, DESPITE HIS LIMITED KNOWLEDGE OF LATIN.

TRISTRAM FINDS LIGHT EXERCISE IN A DUEL OR TWO. IT IS ALL GOOD CLEAN FUN AND NO ONE IS INJURED TOO SERIOUSLY.

183 8-11-40

AS THEY PREPARE TO LEAVE, THE ORIENTAL APPEARS.— "NOBLE SIRS, YE BE KNIGHTS OF TABLE ROUND, BOUND BY OATH TO PUNISH WRONG AND BRING JUSTICE TO THE WEAK... I AM A JEWEL MERCHANT ROBBED OF HALF MY WEALTH BY THE GUARDS I HIRED TO PROTECT ME. EVEN NOW THEY LIE IN WAIT FOR ME ALONG THE ROAD, PLANNING FURTHER ROBBERY. MAY I BEG YOUR PROTECTION UNTIL THAT DANGER IS PAST?"

NEXT WEEK—
Let the Punishment Fit the Crime!

Copr. 1940, King Features Syndicate, Inc. World rights reserved.

HAL FOSTER

GUIDO
SAVE THIS STAMP

Prince Valiant

IN THE DAYS OF KING ARTHUR
BY
Harold R Foster

GATEKEEPER
SAVE THIS STAMP

Synopsis: AS TRISTRAM, PRINCE VALIANT AND SIR GAWAIN ARE PREPARING TO LEAVE THE CITY OF RAVENNA, AN ORIENTAL JEWEL MERCHANT TELLS OF BEING ROBBED BY THE GUARDS HE HAD HIRED TO DEFEND HIM AND _____ ASKS THEIR PROTECTION ON THE ROAD ___ TO ROME.

"EVEN NOW, MY UNFAITHFUL SERVANTS WAIT IN THE WILDERNESS BEYOND TO ROB ME OF THE REST OF MY GOODS."

"OUR SWORDS ARE EVER PLEDGED TO DEFEND THE WEAK FROM OPPRESSION," SAYS TRISTRAM, "AND WE WILL AS QUICKLY DIVORCE YOUR HEAD FROM YOUR BODY IF YOU ARE DECEIVING US." SO THEY LET THE MERCHANT TRAVEL WITH THEM.

"LOOK!" CRIES THE MERCHANT, "YONDER BUSHES SHAKE; SOMEONE IS HIDING THERE AND HONEST MEN DON'T HIDE."

STRIDING INTO THE THICKET, VAL FINDS A CAMPING PLACE, BUT ITS OCCUPANTS ARE FLEEING INTO THE SWAMP BEYOND.

VAL TAKES TWO LEATHERN BUCKLERS FROM THE SQUIRES AND BINDS THEM TO HIS FEET.......

...AND C_____ THE QUAK___ PURSUIT C___ THIEVES.

SIR GAWAIN WATCHES VAL ROUND UP THE FUGITIVES AND HERD THEM BACK. "THE YOUNG PRINCE IS A LIGHTHEARTED SCATTER-BRAIN," HE SAYS "UNTIL A CRISIS COMES; THEN SO MANY TRICKS, SCHEMES AND IDEAS FILL HIS HEAD IT HUMS LIKE A BEE-HIVE!"

WITH ALL HIS GLITTERING MERCHANDISE RESTORED TO HIM, THE ORIENTAL RAISES HIS ARMS IN SILENT THANKS TO THE STRANGE GODS OF HIS DISTANT HOME.

Copr. 1940, King Features Syndicate, Inc., World rights reserved.

THE PUNISHMENT OF THE THIEVES IS LEFT TO THE MOSQUITOES, AS THEY ARE CHASED, NAKED, BACK INTO THE SWAMP.

184 8-18-40

NEXT WEEK— **Crossing the Rubicon.**